Art of Celebration
NEW ENGLAND

Published by

PANACHE
PANACHE PARTNERS

Panache Partners, LLC
1424 Gables Court
Plano, TX 75075
469.246.6060
Fax: 469.246.6062
www.panache.com

Publishers: Brian G. Carabet and John A. Shand

Printed in Malaysia

Distributed by Independent Publishers Group
800.888.4741

PUBLISHER'S DATA

Art of Celebration New England

Library of Congress Control Number: 2010938657

ISBN 13: 978-1-933415-95-6
ISBN 10: 1-933415-95-9

First Printing 2011

10 9 8 7 6 5 4 3 2 1

Panache Partners, LLC is dedicated to the restoration and conservation of the environment. Our books are manufactured with strict adherence to an environmental management system in accordance with ISO 14001 standards, including the use of paper from mills certified to derive their products from well-managed forests. We are committed to continued investigation of alternative paper products and environmentally responsible manufacturing processes to ensure the preservation of our fragile planet.

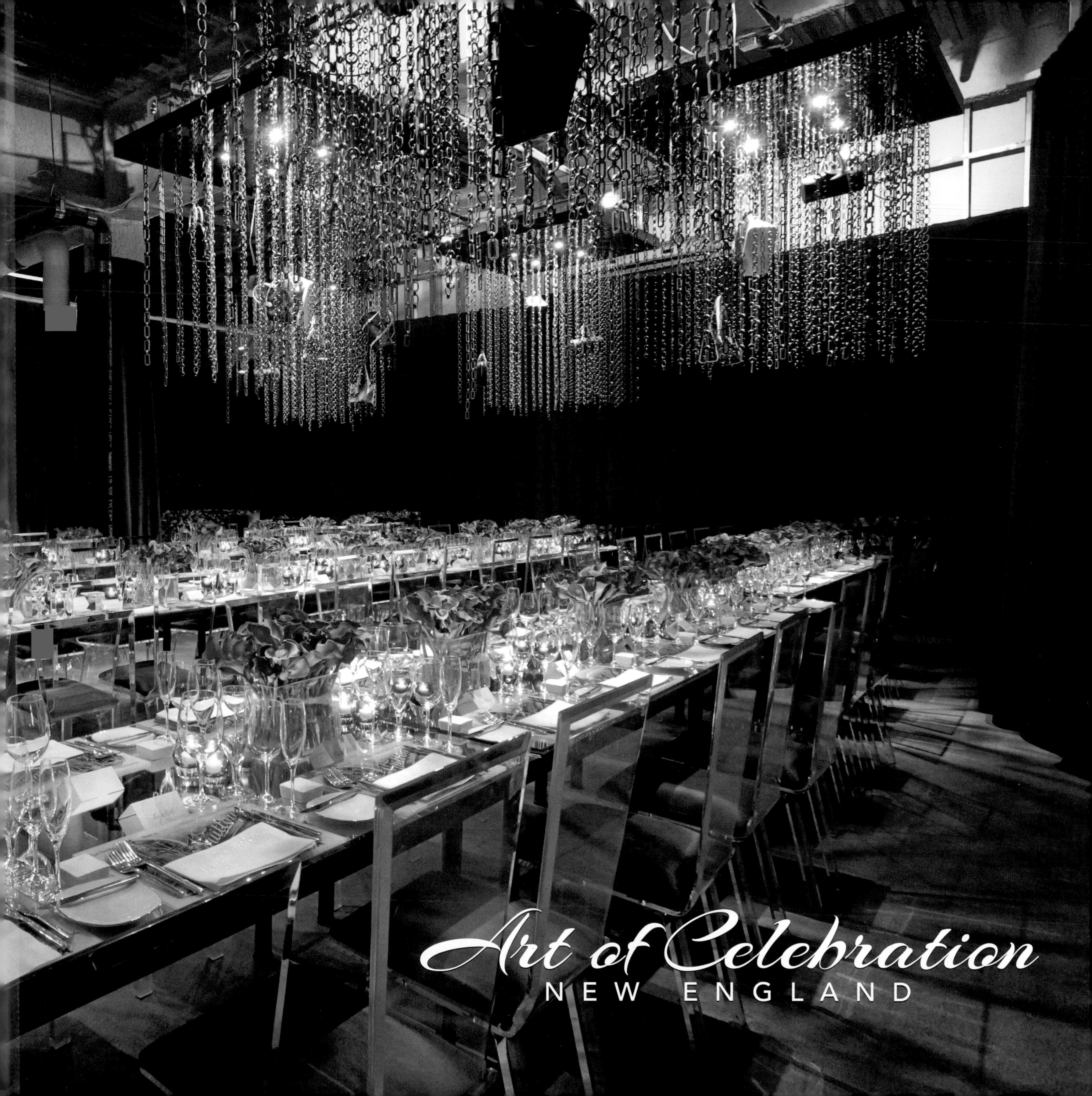
Art of Celebration
NEW ENGLAND

INTRODUCTION

Celebrations are woven into our lives from the moment we are born; we pave our long and winding road with revelry. Cultures are identified by their milestones, rites of passage, and faiths. From the visions of a select few, through the work of many, and motivated by all, our celebrations are universal.

In *Art of Celebration New England*, we chart the area's modern-day visionaries who mastermind remarkable events, creating everlasting memories.

The magic of a phenomenal celebration is achieved with great collaboration. This book will take you on a journey, sharing the insights and creations of the gifted. We begin this journey with event planners—the directors and producers—who pull it all together, manage and execute the visions even BEFORE THE MUSIC BEGINS. And once you've set the date, the next step is LOCATION, LOCATION, LOCATION, so we turn our focus to New England's most incredible venues, which become inspirational backdrops.

The event, floral, and lighting designers are true visionaries of CREATING AN AMBIENCE; these artists are responsible for endless ideas and boundless efforts and are often the heart and soul of an unforgettable gala. Then EAT, DRINK & BE MERRY in the culinary world of caterers, whose works of art and ingenious creations delight the palate and astound the mind. From there, IT'S ALL IN THE DETAILS. Through the amazing talents of musicians, entertainers, photographers, and videographers, CAPTURING THE MOMENT will forever keep alive the experiences of life's ritual—the art of celebration.

Art of Celebration New England will inspire, inform, and just might take your breath away!

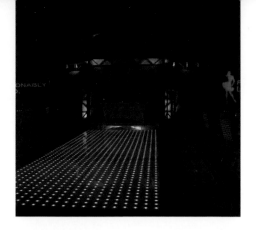

BEFORE THE MUSIC BEGINS

LOCATION, LOCATION, LOCATION

CREATING AN AMBIENCE

CONTENTS

EAT, DRINK & BE MERRY

IT'S ALL IN THE DETAILS

CAPTURING THE MOMENT

MS. DEBBIE COSTELLO
& GUEST
the dreaming tree

5

MR. STEV[E]
& GUEST
up an[d]

"Event planners are the playwrights
of the party."

—Michele Mottola

"For those few hours, your guests are the stars of the show."

—Catherine Stephens

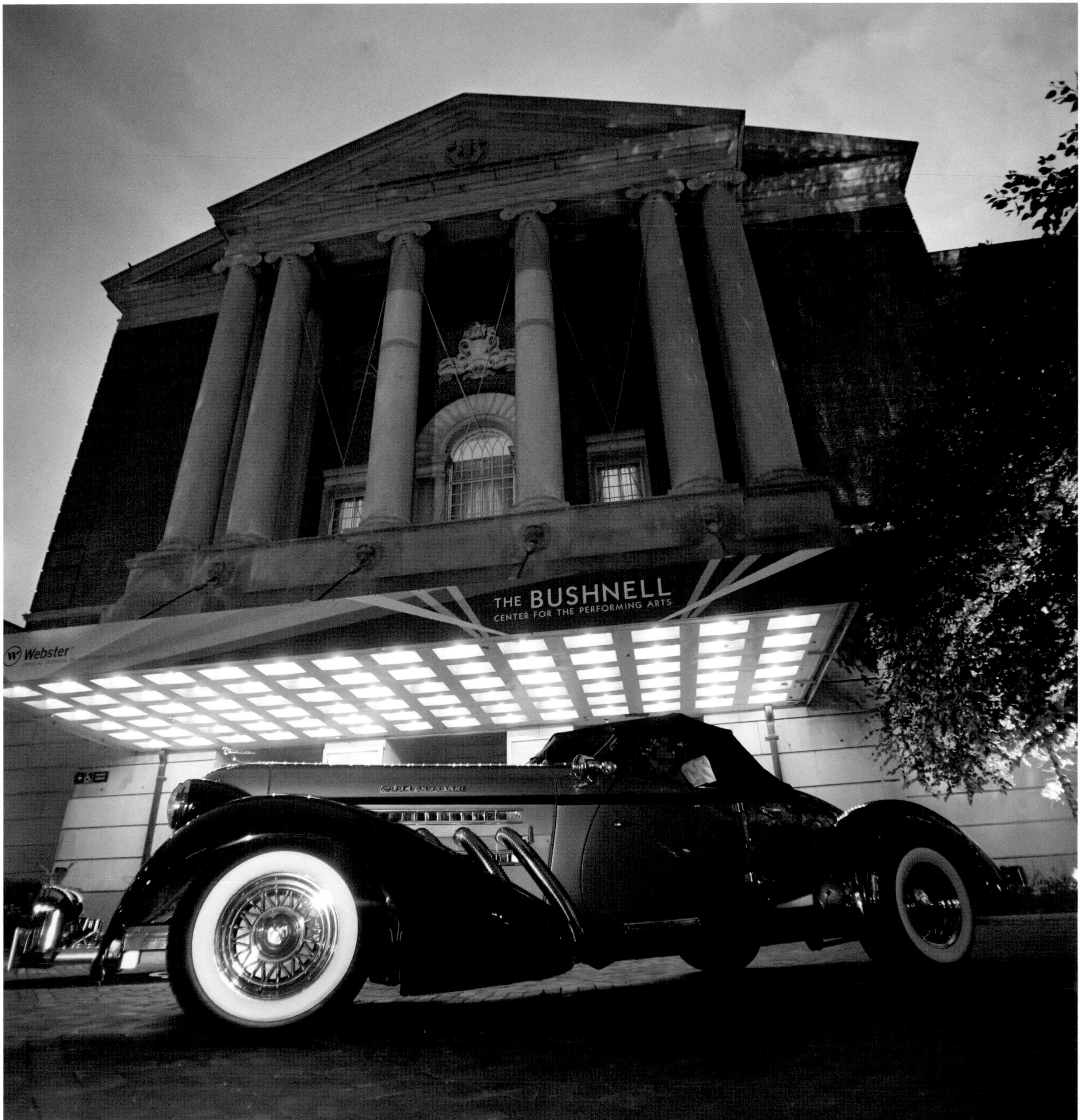
THE BUSHNELL
CENTER FOR THE PERFORMING ARTS
Webster

Before the

Music Begins

RAFANELLI EVENTS

BRYAN RAFANELLI

"Anything is possible" is Bryan Rafanelli's working philosophy. The Rafanelli Events team members are like masterful magicians; they can bring in a baby elephant, erect a glass tent, cast a celebrity chef, and orchestrate a romantic dove release after a nuptial ceremony. A progressive imagineer and entrepreneur, Bryan has been in the business of creating once-in-a-lifetime experiences, producing high-profile social, nonprofit, and corporate celebrations on behalf of Boston's trendsetters and tastemakers since 1996.

Bryan believes that designing and producing an event—whether a bar mitzvah ceremony, anniversary party, charity gala, or luxury store grand opening—is all about telling a story. Hosts who aren't sure of exactly what they want fuel Bryan's creativity to invent an amazingly new and unique experience for guests. His firm is most passionate about the visual concept of an event, but creative director Billy Evers consistently designs each celebration within specified monetary parameters. At Rafanelli Events new ideas flow daily and up to 100 events are designed, produced, and executed to perfection annually. The illustrious firm caters to elite clientele throughout Boston and along the entire East Coast. Bryan and his cadre of creative thinkers present viable options so each celebration reflects the host's objectives. Everyone is immersed in the unfolding creative process, enjoying the planning of details and the professional collaboration, as Rafanelli's vision becomes both an artistic interpretation and a narrative of the event.

Like a diamond in the rough, we transformed raw retail space into a luxury brand celebration.
Our custom mirrored tables reflected our handcrafted mirrored chandeliers, each boasting Louis
Vuitton handbags suspended as eye candy.

Photograph by Matt Teuten Photography

Above and right: Lionel Richie performed for a private anniversary party we produced at the Liberty National Golf Club in New Jersey. We projected imagery onto the ceiling of the tent using state-of-the art technology to turn it into a moving screen of exotic orchids. Guests also enjoyed views of the Statue of Liberty on the opposite shore.

Facing page: We designed the Louis Vuitton boutique's grand opening soirée for 75 guests to be sexy, slick, bright, and inviting with every single detail executed flawlessly.

"You are the master of your celebration."
—Bryan Rafanelli

Above: Our team designed an indoor-outdoor holiday party with an unexpected theme twist. Family and friends were invited for a winter solstice celebration at the hosts' 170-acre private residence. The historic farmhouse replete with fresh snowfall was the perfect canvas for the colorful illumination of crescent moons and stars. A blazing three-story bonfire and enchanting horse-drawn sleigh rides topped off the night.

Facing page: The annual charity gala for the Boston Public Library Foundation met huge success. Party on the Plaza was held in Boston's architecturally rich Copley Square. We designed a custom superstructure right in the soul of the city with a red carpet leading VIPs into a most unexpected venue. Our clear-topped tent allowed guests to enjoy the glittering Boston skyline all evening long.

"Your event should tell a story through the venue, theme, lighting, and décor."

—Bryan Rafanelli

Right: Our summer bar mitzvah party had brick pathways that we lined with trickling fountains to connect the outdoor space to the indoor lounge; we further defined the lounge area with rattan furniture and sculptural twig pendant lighting.

Facing page: Attention to details helped make the 50th birthday party something unforgettable. We set up a tent pavilion on a private estate in Chestnut Hill and extended the lush garden setting by creating a green theme. For an organic feeling, a textured sisal rug replaced typical linens. Unique tabletop décor featured geometric plates and copper candle lanterns.

Photograph by Person + Killian Photography

For the past decade we have enjoyed designing the annual Storybook Ball gala to benefit the Massachusetts General Hospital for Children. Three of these yearly celebrations took place in The Park Plaza Castle, a historic Boston landmark. The old armory building required us to conceal both ceilings and walls with green drapery and cleverly tiled floors to create a fantasy Storybook Ball based on the classic children's book *Peter Pan*. We even framed the video screens to resemble paintings. We transformed the beloved Boston venue once again into a *Mary Poppins*-inspired setting with wraparound screens featuring custom animation. The room's 48-foot-high ceilings with steel rigging points allowed us to have characters fly above dining tables for a theatrical sensation.

Photograph by Matt Teuten Photography

Photograph by Matt Teuten Photography

"The goal is to balance lavishness with enormous value so the event satisfies on all levels."

—Bryan Rafanelli

Right: We designed a couple's 40th anniversary party with VIP access to the New England Patriots' Gillette Stadium with a tent on the 50-yard line for 700 lucky guests. The celebration featured a 180-foot-long red carpet runway with a private concert by Elton John.

Facing page: Our established connections permitted VIP access to Fenway Park's outfield for an exclusive fundraising event themed around the Charlie Brown comic strip. We created a venue within America's oldest baseball field, positioning a glass-sided and clear-topped tent for stunning views of the park with cocktail hour on the warning track. The hospital benefit gala for 600 guests was a big hit.

Photograph by Jeff Crowe

views

Set your sights high, but take a logical approach to your event. Plan ahead and allow up to eight months of lead time, especially if you have a celebrity appearance in mind. Create a timeline, put a guest list together, and make certain it can all realistically happen. Be sure your event partner has exclusive contracts with vendors to secure the best in the business, from custom furniture to world-class entertainment.

HOPPLE POPPLE, INC.

LINDA G. MATZKIN

Hopple popple is a Pennsylvania Dutch tradition, an everything-but-the-kitchen-sink breakfast that combines whatever fared best on the farm that week into an always surprising but always delicious meal. When Linda G. Matzkin set about naming her event planning company over 30 years ago, the concept of a rotating list of seemingly random ingredients uniting into something fantastic appealed to her, and thus Hopple Popple found its name.

However, the company's success in New England has hardly been reliant on gathering concepts and ideas for an event and simply hoping they work. Linda and her team are visionaries, always able to imagine setups, room plans, and tablescapes that draw gasps of ecstatic astonishment from hosts and guests alike. They have planned every sort of event imaginable, making the mundane extraordinary and seemingly impossible events—like ice skating in June—possible.

Discovering one person's taste for the dramatic, another's yearning for formality, and another's proclivity for "going with the flow" is an art which Linda and her coordinators have mastered. The open and animated Hopple Popple offices pulse with energy and creativity, allowing everyone to jump in with a suggestion or nurture an idea to fruition. That sense of collaboration extends to the myriad vendors brought in for any given event. Hopple Popple has established itself as a highly sought-after company for not only would-be hosts, but for florists, caterers, and lighting designers as well. Magically combining dozens of personalities into an event that conveys the taste of one or two hosts is, after all, the very essence behind the notion of Hopple Popple.

The bride and her parents' elegant and gracious taste was reflected throughout the wedding from the moment the guests entered their home. Guests were surrounded by layered terraces and manicured gardens, providing a constant "visual" which extended into the dining tent. Each table was designed to accommodate an exquisite array of china, crystal, candlesticks, and dramatic floral arrangements by my collaborator, the talented floral designer Domenic Cambio. To carry the exquisite décor elements from the home into the tent, Domenic constructed walls of tufted dupioni and custom lacquered tent flooring, each finished in a highly detailed manner.

"Every event is a reflection of the hosts. They have the ideas; we have the tools to make them a reality."
—Linda G. Matzkin

The bride and groom held their tented wedding at the bride's parents' 250-acre orchard. The 48,000-square-foot structure housed every element of the wedding: ceremony, cocktail hour, reception, and afterparty in separate "rooms" draped in diaphanous white fabric. The custom pink-and-white checkered dance floor, where the guests spent most of the night dancing to big band music, was surrounded by heavenly décor including pale pink dupioni linens, heavily beaded organza overlays and chair covers, three different types of china and glassware, and a myriad of crystal floral containers and candleholders. The huppah, architectural in style, was softened by an abundance of phalaenopsis orchids, pale pink and white peonies, and hydrangea, all created and designed by Domenic Cambio. He and I share a multi-dimensional approach which combines his creative genius with my more practical knowledge of the hosts and the endless details of their event.

Photograph by Terry Gruber

Photograph by Terry Gruber

Photograph by Terry Gruber

"The juxtaposition of elegant and edgy, fun and fantasy is what makes event planning challenging and exciting at the same time."

—Linda Matzkin

Photograph by Claudia Kronenberg

Above and right: We created a relaxed but elegant feel inside our clear tent, which was positioned in the center of a golf course. The stark white dance floor, stage, fabric, and flooring with the additional touch of acid green in the linens complemented the white ceramic containers bursting with splashes of colorful flowers. The organic elements in the arrangements helped to bring the outdoors inside.

Facing page: Our "Jane Austen" bride wanted a graceful, formal wedding in the historic Boston Public Library. With its domed ceiling, marble walls, and ornate mouldings, this unique venue was the perfect backdrop for a warm and romantic dinner set with eclectic china patterns and vintage sterling silver containers lush with English garden flowers. Menus and seating cards were scripted in Old English calligraphy, and each guest received a small book with a personalized note from the bride and groom.

Photograph by Claudia Kronenberg

Photograph by The Nourses Photography

Photograph by Claudia Kronenberg

"When hosts are relaxed and comfortable, their guests are relaxed and comfortable—then the fun begins!"

—Linda G. Matzkin

Top: Celebrating graduations—two from high school and one college—meant a party for all ages. The sisters chose a tropical theme so that they could take advantage of the many fun, colorful, fruit-flavored non-alcoholic drinks we could provide in the 40-foot Tiki hut. The structure became the focal point of the party and the watering hole for everyone. We used bold color and texture in our linens, centerpieces, chairs, and furniture, and lit the room in juicy, "hot" colors.

Bottom: At the exact same venue as the graduation party, we went the opposite direction and created a sleek and refined post-wedding celebration. The feel was modern and contemporary, with a monochromatic color scheme of white, taupe, and cream that was carried through the furniture, linens, flowers, and even the floor and walls. Beautifully lit in hues of violet, indigo, and periwinkle, the space absolutely glowed.

Facing page: Using the bride's favorite color palette of plums, eggplants, and fuchsias, we were able to create a multi-layered color experience. With clusters of lanterns lighting the trees, guests were able to appreciate the fall foliage and exquisite grounds. Three-sided pin spots and multiple candles on each table accentuated the varying hues of the high and low floral centerpieces. Who knew there were so many shades of purple!

"No two people are alike, so no two events should be alike."
—Linda G. Matzkin

Right: Our bride and groom wanted a true Nantucket feel to their wedding. The many patterns of blue and white blended perfectly with the ocean and beach views and created an exquisite backdrop for the bursts of color in the flowers. Many details—some subtle, some not so—such as the shell print napkins with hemp rings, "Nantucket red" floral containers, and etched glass chargers with a fish motif added just the right touch. The flowers flawlessly mimicked the famous Nantucket red color, and combined with bright blue hydrangea and other bold-colored flowers, the low arrangements appeared lush and abundant. Sand-colored sisal tent carpeting and parchment ceiling lanterns enhanced the relaxed, elegant feel.

Facing page: A celebration expressing the birthday gal's love of food, fun, and flowers was fabulous in every way. Guests were seated at 40-foot-long tables surrounding a round black dance floor, the design of which mirrored the vibrant colors of the linens and flowers designed by Domenic Cambio. Chefs prepared and presented each course tableside, coupling interaction with entertainment throughout the evening.

Photograph by Geneviève de Manio

views

Consider how all of the elements will work together in a room. Where buffets, bars, and tables are placed, how seating is maximized, how "dreamy" the dance floor looks, how exciting the stage appears, how the room "feels" when the guests arrive—all are questions that need to be answered for a fabulous party.

CREATIVE EVENTS

AJ WILLIAMS

The basic definition of creativity is the discovery of new ideas or concepts, but AJ Williams and her company, Creative Events, are anything but basic. With an incredible grasp of strategy and an endless supply of innovation, AJ and her team have the ability to examine their hosts—whether corporate, nonprofit, or social—and translate their needs into jaw-dropping holiday galas, summer outings, celebrity chef and wine dinners, conferences, corporate roll-outs, festivals, charity and citywide events, weddings, and product and media launches. AJ's thoughtful approach to the event process guarantees that no matter what has been produced before, her vision will be fresh, effective, and exciting.

Creative Events knows how to take the reins on any event and steer it to success from start to finish. Managing everything from the venue, production, and logistics to the publicity, graphic design, and décor means that AJ can truly provide an all-encompassing brand design that ties it all together. Identifying and securing unique fundraising and sponsorship opportunities, as well as coordinating high-profile entertainment, has resulted in nonprofit events that have surpassed all previous incarnations.

With a client list that includes such bold-face names as Hill Holiday, Blue Cross Blue Shield of Massachusetts, Arbella Insurance, BeanTown Jazz Fest, Harvard Business School, and Saks Fifth Avenue, Creative Events has the experience and contacts to make virtually anything a reality. By combining modern trends with strategy and elegant design, Creative Events can plan the ultimate event.

For a sweet 16 party, the birthday girl really wanted to incorporate her two favorite things: fashion and the color pink. We handled all the creative aspects of the event, from the linens and flowers to graphic design and a personalized logo that adorned every printed element.

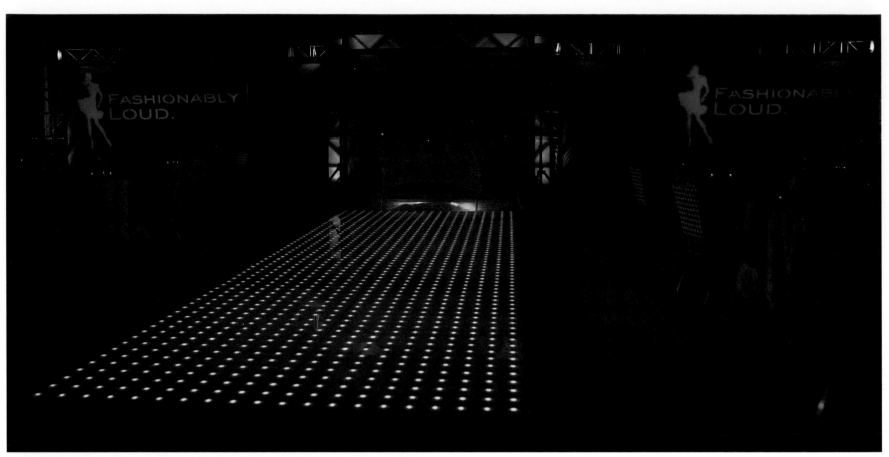

Photograph by David Fox Photographer

Above and left: We wanted these girls to feel like true fashionistas, so they began the evening by walking the "pink carpet" before being interviewed on video by local personalities. Inside, they received flutes of sparkling cider and enjoyed hors d'oeuvres on the balcony overlooking the Liberty Hotel's active and trendy lobby before heading downstairs for the fashion show. The girls strutted down a runway lit by pulsating, flickering LED lights, feeling all the while like gorgeous supermodels.

Facing page top left: A holiday party at the State Room with a Latin theme was meant to emphasize community, exemplified by Spanish fusion tapas plates prepared by chef Ken Oringer and professional salsa dancers who performed and engaged guests on the dance floor. The warm, inviting lounge atmosphere was enhanced by amber lighting and birch-paneled walls.

Facing page bottom left: Arrangements by Winston Flowers, white tufted furniture brought in from New York City, and iridescent organdy draped around the room gave the space a hip, contemporary feel.

Facing page right: The first year we worked with the BeanTown Jazz Festival, the daily attendance jumped from 10,000 to 30,000 people on Saturday alone; over the next few years attendance grew to over 75,000. Through fundraising and sponsorship opportunities, we have helped turn the festival into a multi-day event encompassing over 100 exhibitors.

Photograph courtesy of High Output

Photograph by AJ Williams

Photograph by AJ Williams

Queen Latifah, Jennifer Hudson, Michael McDonald—we've been able to secure some pretty incredible headliners to entertain at nonprofit events over the years. Not only have they helped significantly with ticket sales and publicity, but their mere presence lends an aura of magic to the entire event. People love to see celebrities perform in person, and if they are lending their support to a particular cause, it aids that organization in more ways than you can imagine.

Photograph by Eric Antoniou Photography

"By looking inside the box to identify what was executed in the past, you can strategically think outside the box to produce events that maximize impact on all levels."

—AJ Williams

Design Industries Foundation Fighting AIDS launched a terrific event called Dining by Design, where design professionals were asked to construct vignettes to invite people to dine and donate to a great cause. My design was actually influenced by a George Michael concert. I replicated the curved lines of the digitally-controlled stage in the dining room table that I had custom-made, and the pewter glass balls of the chandelier reminded me of flashbulbs. After the showcase, a guest actually bought the table, the chandelier, and the birch bark as a wallpaper for their dining room, something that's virtually unheard of.

Photograph by Eric Antoniou Photography

views

It's all about the trend-setting details that guests will talk about for months. Using a combination of strategy, creating anticipation for the event, precise attention to details, and adding smart marketing messages to creative environments, your event will be both thoughtful and well executed—no matter what type of event.

EXQUISITE EVENTS
STASIA ANTHONY | KELLI DUBEAU

Some people see those working in their same industry not as competitors, but as possible partners. Stasia Anthony, fresh from coordinating in-house entertainment and corporate events for Citibank in New York City, arrived in Newport, Rhode Island, in the early 1990s and quickly formed Glorious Affairs, a thriving catering business. Kelli DuBeau was working as the Newport Naval Officer's Club's social secretary, introducing the club to formal tented events and igniting her interest in the decorating medium. After 11 years she branched out on her own and opened The Main Event, quickly becoming the leading expert in interior tent décor and ambient lighting. In 2002, the ladies joined creative forces and Exquisite Events was born.

Now they work as an unstoppable team, planning and designing over 100 events yearly around New England and beyond. Kelli's rare mix of resourcefulness, imagination, and style has paired perfectly with Stasia's flexibility, creativity, and organizational skills. Merging their respective pasts has given them the opportunity to tackle larger and more complicated events, while still lending their signature touch to small and intimate gatherings.

Within her 10,000-square-foot warehouse, Kelli's team can build, assemble, personalize, or scout just about any prop, piece of furniture, or lighting fixture. Everything from a 19-foot-tall Eiffel Tower to a leather lounge vignette to mountains of fabric resides there. In the office, Stasia meets with her hosts, carefully detailing every aspect of their event plans so that when the big day arrives, every element is exquisite.

We're big believers in complementing your venue, so even though the ceremony was originally planned to be held outdoors at The Breakers Palm Beach, weather dictated we set up in the ballroom. It pays to always have a plan B ready that can equal or sometimes even surpass the original plan A.

Photograph by Rebecca Bouck

For various reasons, the couple had planned their wedding three different times in three different locations. Each time the theme and feel changed dramatically, but there were always elements of elegance and drama. Richard Grille and The Design Studio at The Breakers used contemporary aspects and lighting techniques to create a modern feel in an opulent environment.

"Every person has a unique perspective that will take a design in its own direction."
—Kelli DuBeau

It is possible to delineate more than one space within a tent. On one end, a soft, romantic dining area overflowed with rich colors, gauzy linens, and a fireworks explosion of flowers. Separated by a draped "wall," the modern club atmosphere offered guests a place to mingle and lounge on hip white leather furniture. The next tent recreated a Mexican cantina, complete with hammered copper lanterns, a mariachi band, and buckets brimming with Corona long-necks.

Photograph by Snap!

Photograph by Snap!

Photograph by Priscilla Malone

"It's invaluable to have a team who understands how each other works and is constantly striving for perfection."

—Stasia Anthony

Right: A birthday party for a woman who was extremely involved with her local animal shelter allowed us to mesh a truly gorgeous outdoor dinner setting with a fun and whimsical theme. Guests dined under a pergola covered in vines and flowers that was strung with hundreds of hanging candles, mirroring the candles that also floated in the pool and were placed around the property. Hand-illustrated placecards were themed to each particular guest, showing Chihuahuas, dachshunds, and other puppies that held special significance.

Facing page: Truly timeless designs always present a crisp and clean look. Celery-colored linens paired with antique white chandeliers and chairs unified the mix of Tuscan booths and round tables.

Photograph by Exquisite Events

views

Experience does make an enormous difference in both the design and orchestration of an event. The more your event planner has seen and dealt with, the better equipped she is to handle whatever might be thrown her way leading up to or during your event.

MICHELE MOTTOLA SPECIAL EVENTS CONSULTING
MICHELE MOTTOLA

Some event planners are known for their invisibility, a talent for orchestrating festivities behind the scenes. Unlike most, Michele Mottola can be found right in the thick of things on both sides of the event. Coordinating the arrival and responsibilities of multiple vendors or freeing a bride from her too-snug sheepskin boot—she's comfortable doing either. But one thing she never does is pull the curtain back on the magic. Running flawless events and extinguishing unexpected minor or major wrinkles that pop up are just a few of the many things Michele is revered for.

Michele's proactive planning goes far beyond organizing the event. From the first consultation she lays it all out, providing her clients with as much information as they need or want so that their minds can rest easy throughout the planning process and on through the event. Keeping the months leading up to their event organized, professional, stress-free, and—gasp!—fun is a Michele Mottola trademark.

Her experience working with New England's most respected vendors also speaks volumes. When Michele, a two-decade veteran of prestigious luxury hotel brands, makes a request, floral designers, caterers, and lighting specialists bend over backwards to accommodate. They know that Michele will have considered every detail necessary to make sure the event runs smoothly, and that the experience will be not only enjoyable, but anxiety-free.

A bride from Alabama wanted her reception to be held under a grove of peach trees, but as the site was indoors and in Boston, Marc Hall constructed a dramatic canopy of towering southern magnolia branches and Suzanne B. Lowell's lighting design shimmered over a collection of glass vessels brimming with orchid blossoms.

A snowy winter's evening, crackling fire pits, Belgian draft horses, and a cozy reception inside of a rustic barn—those are the ingredients for a wedding weekend designed around pure rustic elegance. The masculine yet stylized palette of light grey, white, steel, and dark brown was reflected in the two 24-foot-long family-style tables, beautifully lit by Suzanne B. Lowell Lighting Design. Custom iron chandeliers hovered just above the guests' sightline, dripping with glass and botanical accents from Marc Hall. We brought color in through the cocktails: a hibiscus daiquiri poured into an aqua diamond-cut martini glass, and to balance it out, a bourbon Old Fashioned served in a retro, heavy-bottomed glass. Although the outcome was magical, the event did have its share of hurdles, like the fact that one of the horses turned out to be afraid of fire!

Above and left: There is a lot of juxtaposition in what I do. I love to mix sleek lines with natural beauty, contemporary touches within a traditional base. Showcasing lemons and jasmine within an acrylic shadow box table and then topping it with manzanita tree chips sculpted into a massive structure adorned with hand-crafted butterflies brought in a woodsy, organic feeling.

Facing page: I encourage my hosts to never feel pressured to follow trends. When you look back on your event, whether it was a wedding, birthday celebration, anniversary, or family gathering, you want to see yourself reflected in the décor, not whatever theme or color was popular that year.

Photograph by David Tucker

TO LOAD
SKI POLES IN
RT. HAND
STAND ON
MARK
LOOK OVER LT.
SHOULDER
SIT DOWN
LOSE SAFETY
ATE

Photograph by David Tucker

Photograph by David Tucker

Photograph by David Tucker

"Event planners are the playwrights of the party."

—Michele Mottola

Often Fourth of July parties fall victim to traditional themes, but with creative thinking I was able to blend time-honored traditions with unique contemporary elements. Welcoming guests with a personalized bucket full of local goodies set the relaxed yet festive tone, and by the time the delicious family-style dinner of lobster, clams, mussels, filet mignon, corn-on-the-cob, and truffle oil French fries was served, everyone was already having a blast. Gigantic hand-wired lighted orbs from Italy, courtesy of Suzanne B. Lowell Lighting Design, made the crystal tent's interior sparkle but didn't detract from the fireworks display that capped off the night.

views

Knowing that everything has been methodically planned allows you to live in the moment and truly enjoy the event. Although every detail is important, nothing is more important than enjoying the company of your guests and the party you worked so hard to create. That's precisely why I am there: to allow the process I created to unfold so that you never lose sight of that.

AMBIANCE CHIC WEDDING DESIGNS

ERICA ELIZABETH KATES

Interior designers create rooms that are enjoyed day-in and day-out for years, while event designers create magical spaces that are lived in for only a matter of hours but live on in photographs and cherished memories. Erica Elizabeth Kates began her career designing residential interior spaces, and her exploratory nature propelled her to try her hand at wedding planning and design. She founded Ambiance Chic Wedding Designs with the aim of promoting the spirit of collaboration—both within her company and with the hosts she works with. Along with her primary planners and event team, Erica brings a fresh twist to every event.

By utilizing every team member's unique perspective and ideas, Ambiance Chic can dream up an inventive approach to nearly every aspect of an event. Known as the forces behind the wonderfully quirky design of the first same-sex marriage to be featured in *Martha Stewart Weddings* magazine, Erica and her team of "traveling artists" have quickly and notably been making a name for themselves in the New England event scene.

The ambition of the Ambiance team is translating each aspect of their host's personality into everything from the linens and flowers to the candleholders. When helping to select vendors, Ambiance Chic leans toward photographers, entertainment, paper designers, and floral designers known not only for their impeccable reputation but for also having a style that would best suit their host. Truly reflecting what makes each couple unique is Ambiance Chic's key to unforgettable events.

Remember to look at your event from three angles: the big, the immediate, and the small. Keep the big picture in mind and make sure everything supports the overall design scheme. Know what you and your guests are going to notice immediately upon entering a space. Think hard about the tiny details: the things that may not catch someone's eye at first but are ultimately what give your event personality.

Photograph by Danny Kash Photography

Photograph by Danny Kash Photography

New England is the perfect setting for "antique chic" design, one of the specialties of the Ambiance team. This is a terrific opportunity to bring in personal materials that may not fit into a stricter design scheme. Working with Candice Millard of Candi's Floral Creations, we combined naturally inspired floral arrangements with an assortment of found objects. A vintage sofa, antique vessels, ceramic birds, metal mailbox numbers, and even a vase belonging to the bride's grandmother gave the event character. Using something that you find in an antique shop, barn, yard sale, or even borrow from a family member is eclectic design. Pulling everything together with a well thought out color scheme gives this look a high level of design.

"You've succeeded when an event reflects the best version of each idea."

—Erica Elizabeth Kates

"'Bold' can mean a saturated color palette or a collection of unique materials that together create a dazzling overall effect."

—Erica Elizabeth Kates

An enchanted forest wedding that drew its inspiration from peacock feathers translated the bird's exotic presence into every aspect of the wedding, including the flowers from Candi's Floral Creations. Preceded by flower girls wearing custom-designed fairy wings, bridesmaids carried candlelit lanterns festooned with feathers, ribbons, and jewels down the aisle. Even the bride's shoes—which I embellished in my design studio—gave a cheeky nod to peacocks and enchantment.

Photograph by Michelle Wade Photography

views

Creativity has no limits. By choosing a magnificent event planner and trusting them to help you make deliberate choices, it is absolutely possible to pull off a gorgeous, personally inspired, and imaginative event.

DESTINATION AFFAIRS

KRISTIN CHAMBERS

When you're planning an event, the amount of information you have to keep track of is staggering. But what if your event also involves travel? How do you choose a destination that is right for your event? Who do you rely on to coordinate hotel, airfare, and ground transportation for you and your guests? And what about finding those once-in-a-lifetime activities or locals-only spots that guidebooks and websites haven't discovered? Kristin Chambers of Destination Affairs not only knows how to pull together a fabulous event, but she can do it just about anywhere in the world.

A professional hospitality veteran with an insatiable appetite for travel, Kristin decided to merge her two passions. She offers an experience that helps hosts and guests alike enjoy every moment of an important event without worrying about the necessary but often energy-sapping hassles of travel. Besides making getting to and from an event a flawless occurrence, Kristin and her profoundly experienced team pool their own knowledge and experiences to unearth the most memorable locations and outings, whether they be in Boston, New York, Italy, Hawaii, Spain, Thailand, or Hong Kong.

What the team at Destination Affairs does transcends the terms "travel agent" and "event planner." They are instead specialty travel consultants and event managers who work with both hosts and guests to handcraft a personal itinerary that's perfect for them. A funky, speakeasy-inspired party in Quebec or a relaxed Tuscan wedding complete with pizza making and wine tasting—no matter the continent, country, or city, Destination Affairs can find a way to make it even more memorable.

When you're traveling, you may not initially be as willing to take risks with your event. Having someone who is knowledgeable about a destination—from its luxury worldwide brands to the quaint mom-and-pop establishments—helps put your mind at ease and gives you the confidence to try something new with the design, cuisine, or type of excursions you plan.

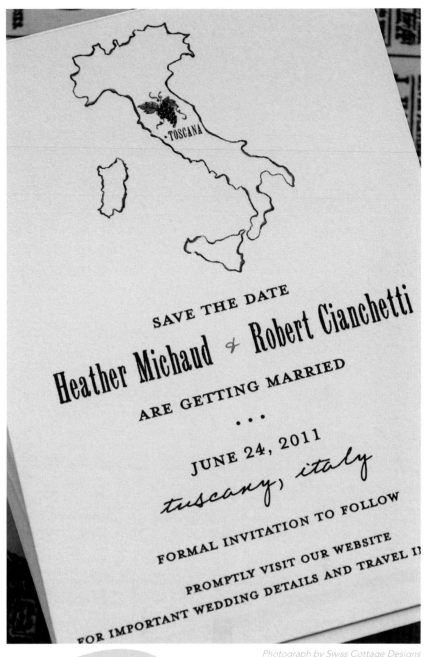

Photograph by Swiss Cottage Designs

"It's easier than you think to bring your local worldwide."

—Kristin Chambers

I love opportunities to meet new people and experience different local cultures. It's my responsibility to maintain relationships with everyone from the chefs and the event coordinators at a high-end resort in Santorini to the cab driver in Cabo San Lucas who knows every happening spot in the city. By knowing about each location's history and culture, I can create and authenticate enjoyable experiences abroad.

views

Destination events are becoming more and more popular. Guests are thrilled to seize the opportunity to explore an exotic locale they may have never visited before and celebrate with friends and family. If guests choose to extend their stay longer and continue exploring, make sure they are in good hands with your destination manager.

NEWPORT HOSPITALITY

LAURIE Z. STROLL

The ultimate way to experience a destination involves more than just a brochure and a disposable camera—it involves an authentic slice of everything the place has to offer with respect to local culture, cuisine, and history. Newport Hospitality is an accredited destination management company and guides groups from start to finish, from accommodations and transportation to all outside activities and special events. Laurie Stroll, who's been in the hospitality industry most of her life, started with Newport Hospitality in 1992 and took over ownership in 2004. She continues to build its professional reputation and connect with Newport's cozy community, local vendors, and family-owned businesses.

The vision of the person booking the event is very important, so Laurie begins the planning process by uncovering as much information as possible about the participants: who they are, where they are from, what their interests are, and why they are coming to Newport. For a true New England experience, Laurie likes to get visitors out on the water—whether for an activity or dinner—and introduce them to Rhode Island's 400 miles of glorious coast, inland scenery, museums, mansions, and other regionally flavored sites.

The friendly staff members' intimate knowledge of the area saves event hosts time, money, and stress. They take care of all the little things—from making sure vendors are insured to communicating every minute detail and always staying one step ahead. When challenges arise, being well respected goes a long way in finding solutions, especially in a small community.

To celebrate the 60th anniversary of the lifestyle brand GANT, the company brought in their global leadership teams from more than 20 countries. The goal of the celebration was to recreate an authentic New England experience to communicate their core brand values. We began the day with chartered 12-meter America's Cup yachts for a regatta up the Narragansett Bay to The Carnegie Abbey Club and ended with an authentic clam and lobster bake.

Photograph by Meghan Sepe

Photograph by Meghan Sepe

Photograph by Meghan Sepe

Photograph by Meghan Sepe

"Having a clambake overlooking the water while boats sail by really has a way of allowing people to slow down, relax, and enjoy."

—Laurie Z. Stroll

After an invigorating afternoon of racing for glory, guests were greeted by servers with a tray of the club's signature cocktail, The Carnegie Sunset—a delicate blend of aged brandy and fresh blackberries topped with champagne. A traditional Rhode Island clambake followed, complete with an informative talk given by the clambake master. After s'mores around the fire pit, trolleys transported guests back to their hotel. The following evening, guests attended a jazz reception on the terrace at Marble House mansion overlooking the water and the Chinese Tea House. A formal dinner was served in the ballroom with beautiful piano music.

views

There is no obstacle or unforeseeable challenge that can't be overcome. Our job is to make a flawless event look easy. We accomplish this by working with the best in the business and those we know we can trust.

SD Events

TASHA BRACKEN

Boutique event planning agency SD Events isn't New England's largest firm, but its impressive portfolio proves that you don't have to be big to be the best. For more than eight years, SD Events has designed and executed memorable affairs the world over, expertly transforming people's visions into unique and engaging experiences that they and their guests will remember for a lifetime. Beginning with the concept, SD Events draws on its ever-expanding network of professional resources, assembling a team of event professionals that perfectly aligns with each host's personality. In this sense, the ladies of SD are matchmakers, not only facilitating the logistics of an event but ensuring that the experience is smooth and enjoyable.

Recognized in numerous New England and national publications and television and radio programs, the ladies who comprise SD Events are right at home creating any event. From the most intimate dinner to the most elaborate destination wedding at Costa Rica's El Castillo de Esparza, which has chosen SD to be its exclusive event planner, Tasha Bracken, Tricia Frederico, and Stephanie Rossi are there every step of the way. They simplify the process and address every detail, leaving you free to do what's really important: have a fabulous time!

One of the most powerful ways to create atmosphere at an event is with color. Contrasting bold colors, like pink, magenta, and chocolate brown, creates a modern, sensually engaging environment. Bringing out the color palette with the lighting, place settings, and flora immerses guests in the ambience and sets just the right mood.

"A good designer will work with you to understand and execute your vision. The design should feel fresh and fun—a reflection of you."
—Tasha Bracken

Right: The venue plays an important role in shaping the event's design. In New England, we're blessed with a variety of excellent entertainment spaces, from classic to contemporary. Choosing fabric, flora, and lighting that complement and draw attention to the architecture brings the venue to life and establishes a real sense of place and time.

Facing page: As important as the vision is an event's wow factor. This can be achieved in many ways, but often a dramatic detail is all you need. Smaller gatherings allow for more elaborate design elements, such as an intricate fabric and floral chair covering. Larger events necessitate a simpler, equally evocative statement. Votives at various heights can cast a softening glow while underscoring a modern, geometric aesthetic, and a bold floral centerpiece can create simple sophistication.

views

Establish your budget and guest list before you begin looking for a venue. Doing so will help narrow your focus and make the selection process much easier. If you decide on a tented event at your home, keep in mind that while beautiful, it can also be very tricky, as you'll need to provide all the things a hotel has built in. Evaluate your property to determine whether you have access to electrical outlets and enough restroom facilities to accommodate your guests.

SIGNATURE EVENTS

AMY PIPER

For Amy Piper, owner and event planner at Signature Events, passion is the foundation of her work. First seen through her entrepreneurial spirit, Amy's zeal created a successful jewelry design business that took advantage of her innate instincts and artistic flair. Her foray into the event industry began with an artisans' showcase called A Gathering of Friends, which she planned and hosted in her 100-year-old farmhouse each Thanksgiving for eight years. This newfound love of planning, a passion for details, and an appreciation for teamwork led to the inception of Signature Events—a full-service event planning firm specializing in weddings, corporate gatherings, and special events—in 1998.

From the floral and lighting design to the style of entertainment, Amy exudes a natural ability to orchestrate these individual aspects into a sensational event. Her carefully cultivated rapport with numerous industry professionals combines perfectly with her ability to provide each event host with the right team of professionals based on the host's individual style, taste, and budget. When the celebration reflects the signature of the host, all the way from the overall ambience down to the tiniest details, then Amy knows she's hit the mark.

Inspired by color, her innovative ideas spin off unique branding, which Amy believes is the key for a cohesive and inviting event. Whether she's involved in every facet of an occasion or simply offers constructive ideas or resources, Amy's creative energy, experience, and attention to detail are essential to the planning process.

Working with a family through multiple events is always an honor and a privilege. For the first wedding, the daughter wanted a lakeside summer celebration. Two years later, a second daughter tied the knot in a Boston hotel during the winter. As guests enjoyed cocktails in the adjacent lobby, Winston Flowers and Be Our Guest were part of the professional team that helped me turn the ceremony into a reception, creating an elegant, sophisticated ambience with just a hint of holiday spirit. Glimmering candlelight, luxurious red amaryllis, and exquisite magnolia leaf enhanced the coordinating low and tall elements on the head table. Ivory napkins, embellished with a rhinestone cuff, were custom-designed to complement the gold rhinestone votives on each table.

Photograph by Signature Events

"Color brings an unrivaled energy to an event."

—Amy Piper

Right: Turquoise Chinese lanterns and specialty lighting effects transformed a tented tennis court into the desired wow factor. A photo of the beloved family pet, a black Labrador retriever, ended up being the source of inspiration for the wedding. A graphic icon of the dog gleefully jumping off a dock was created for the invitation. To brand the wedding with the icon, I integrated the image into the event décor by including it in a custom ice sculpture, the seating chart, custom luminary bags, a gobo on the dance floor, and elegantly engraved brandy glasses designed as favors for the guests.

Facing page: Every detail counts when planning an event. I love to showcase something unique for each event, from custom-designed linens for an elegant, fall-inspired table setting to an initialed banner that has become a timeless tradition at all family events. On other occasions, the distinctive aspects are found simply through creative and innovative food presentation or in a whimsical way to display escort cards.

views

Working with event professionals who are team players is extremely important. With the right collaboration, everyone's goal is the same—to do whatever it takes to make the event a stunning success. An in-depth timeline appropriately paired with flexibility makes the collaborative process go more smoothly, ensuring every element is accounted for and correctly timed for delivery, setup, and execution.

Twist Event Design & Management

LISA LANIADO | ABBY RORDORF

When important occasions warrant unique and memorable celebrations, Lisa Laniado and Abby Rordorf of twist event design & management make sure that each is customized to fully reflect the guest of honor. While they are never afraid to embrace new and unusual ideas, they are always mindful to design what is truly comfortable for the guests. The firm's intimate size means that it can focus on building partnerships with families, relationships that allow for the vision behind the party to be realized in a meaningful way.

As their design boutique nears a decade of success, Lisa and Abby have held true to the essential questions that have informed them from the beginning: What do you want your event to say? What kind of feeling and memories do you want your family to have? Every event has a message, and twist is determined to present it in an elegant and innovative manner. Whether the event they are working on is modest or grand, the designers are intensely focused on innovative concept, a personal approach, and memorable results.

For a bar mitzvah with a Hollywood theme, we designed in an active film studio. Using the space's endless lighting capabilities, projecting movies old and new on the walls, and painting the concrete floor lent drama to the venue. Custom linens and a textured palette of red, gold, and black along with luscious floral added elegance, glamour, and sophistication.

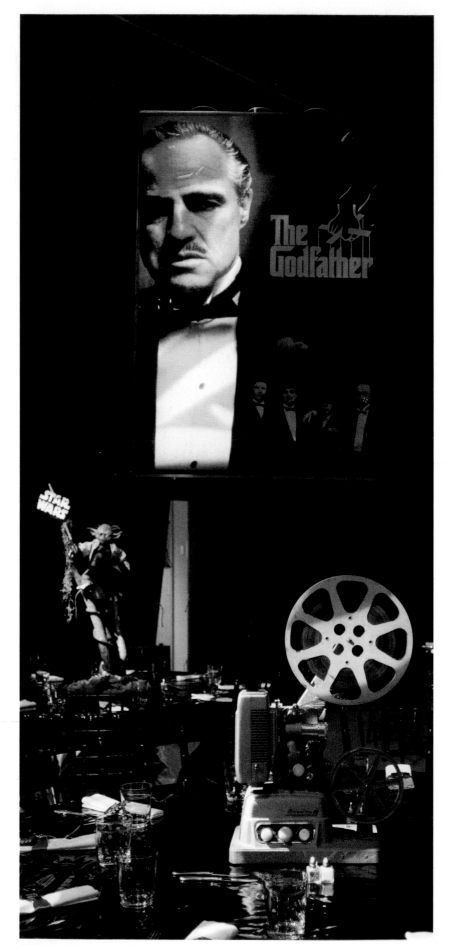

"Allowing imagination to reach its full potential is what vision is all about."
—Abby Rordorf

We brought film to life, infusing the kids' tables with action and fun. Bold centerpieces accentuated by patent leather linen represent the guest of honor's favorite movies. Live gold statues flank the parting-gift table with personalized popcorn boxes and theater-sized candy. Dramatic furniture and orchid chandeliers set the tone for the adults to enjoy sumptuous food and cocktails.

Photograph by Liz Linder Photography

views

Define your signature style while creating an exceptional experience at any budget. The details matter but the overall feeling is what is remembered.

NEWPORT MANSIONS
THE PRESERVATION SOCIETY OF NEWPORT COUNTY

Imagine stepping into the graciousness of Colonial times, the Victorian era, or America's Gilded Age. Rhode Island's renowned Newport Mansions, the 11 historic properties of The Preservation Society of Newport County, are set amid 80 acres of gardens and parks on the breathtaking Atlantic seaboard. Each building has its own regal character: The Breakers, The Elms, Marble House, The Chinese Teahouse, Rosecliff, Château-sur-Mer, Kingscote, Isaac Bell House, Green Animals Topiary Garden, Hunter House, and Chepstow.

Today, a world of exceptional elegance and inspiration in architecture, art, interior design, and landscapes is the perfect backdrop for intimate and large-scale events. Whether attending a wedding, birthday, anniversary celebration, corporate dinner, or gala fundraiser, guests will enjoy the journey back in time at one of America's premier collections of historic house museums. Sip cocktails at The Chinese Teahouse or enjoy a Viennese-style dessert on the fragrant Rosecliff terrace. A celebration at the Newport Mansions promises lasting memories. Philip F. Pelletier serves as the director of special events for The Preservation Society of Newport County, the private, nonprofit institution dedicated to preserving Newport's historic architecture and landscapes.

Designed by architect Stanford White and built in 1902, Rosecliff was modeled after the Grand Trianon of Versailles. The most romantic mansion venue, our spacious 40-by-80-foot ballroom features 22-foot-high ceilings with ornate frieze work reminiscent of icing designs on a classical wedding cake. Exquisite French crystal chandeliers and a wispy blue sky painting give an airy, outdoor impression.

Photograph by Ira Kerns

Above and right: The Rosecliff façade showcases its H-shaped structure and magnificent glazed terracotta exterior. Five sets of French doors open to formal gardens on the west side and out to a gilded fountain and beautiful ocean vista facing east. Pre-dinner cocktail parties under the terrace awning allow guests to enjoy the fountain and elegant grounds. A circular driveway offers a gracious approach to the front entrance.

Facing page: Accommodating up to 200 seated dinner guests, the elegant Rosecliff Ballroom is readily adapted to personal taste through color scheme and décor. The head table, dressed in pink peonies and white roses for a wedding feast, is fit for leaders of society just as the original Oelrichs family residents had intended.

Photograph by Ira Kerns

"Stunning architecture and grounds offer unique options for ceremonies and receptions."

—Philip F. Pelletier

Above and right: American magnates of the early 20th century were fascinated by the Far East. Behind Marble House, The Chinese Tea House is perched above the Cliff Walk, offering panoramic views of the Atlantic Ocean. Alva Vanderbilt entertained friends in The Chinese Tea House for afternoon parties, and also hosted suffrage gatherings there. The intimate space nicely accommodates 50 guests for a seated dinner, 75 people for a standing reception. Our tablescape décor pays homage to Chinese tradition with its symbolic red, green, and white theme.

Facing page: In the foyer of Rosecliff, the sweeping grand staircase forms a heart shape, creating a stunning photo opportunity. Rosecliff at twilight takes on a glamorous appearance for galas year-round. Topiary trees flank the entrance while the Palm Court whispers of the past with scented roses.

"While the gardens and grounds are spectacular in season, historic houses also offer enchanting backdrops for fall and winter events."

—Philip F. Pelletier

Photograph by John Corbett

Above: By suspending red Asian lanterns, we illuminated our tent pavilion for our Dynasties and Dragons dinner-dance gala serving 500 guests. A caterer from our exclusive vendor list was commissioned to create special menus. We work with professional event planners and designers to reflect the celebratory theme from flowers to gourmet food to music.

Facing page: On a beautiful summer night, we hosted our Tiffany Ball, a seated dinner for 400 guests to benefit The Preservation Society of Newport County. Surrounded by immaculate lawns and gardens, the fundraising event was alive with color. Exquisite antique place settings from the original Vanderbilt family estate feature lavish 24-karat gold embellished bone china and gold-plated silverware recalling the epitome of the Gilded Age.

Photograph by John Corbett

Photograph by Richard Cheek

Photograph by Richard Cheek

"There were many extravagant high society parties during the Gilded Age which serve as inspiration for the celebrations hosted today."
—Philip F. Pelletier

Right: The limestone façade of The Elms is reminiscent of a French château. More than 350 guests attended its housewarming party in 1901. The original infrastructure with underground coal delivery rails is intact, yet modern utilities make the property ideal for hosting any event.

Facing page: The Elms estate includes beautiful fountains and gardens. We added candlelight to enhance the nighttime effect and a tent pavilion glows just beyond an enormous weeping beech tree. The conservatory was a favorite room of the Berwind family. Today, cocktail parties are held in the conservatory and adjoining terrace. The Elms' grand foyer creates an impressive entrance with 18th-century Venetian paintings, marble columns, ornate ironwork, and lantern lighting.

Photograph by Patrick O'Connor

views

Advance planning is required when choosing a public museum venue, as evenings are available but some days are closed. The compromises are small when compared to the amazing views and overall satisfaction that a spectacular historic site will provide. Be sure your venue has the ability to tailor your event from catering to antique china to privately guided museum tours, so you can truly have the party of your dreams.

"Impeccable attention to details and flawless service should apply as much to the venue as to any other event component."

—Erwin Schinnerl

Top and facing page: The Ballroom was designed to be versatile in its décor. Silver leaf ceilings, luxurious silk wallcoverings, and custom-designed carpet can stand alone with only the simplest of adornment or can carry the weight of a complete transformation. Top event designed by Hopple Popple.

Bottom: Having an event in The Hamilton Room denotes utter privacy, as it and The Washington Room are essentially in their own wing of the hotel. A pre-function space ideal for cocktails connects the two rooms, which are perfectly designed for smaller parties.

Photograph by Corinne Schippert Photography

Photograph by Drew Hyman

"Sometimes a hotel can intertwine with a city's history, resulting in the magical feeling of being a part of something momentous."

—Erwin Schinnerl

Right: A mother-of-pearl wall is one of those decadent touches that make an event space truly unforgettable.

Facing page: A spring-themed luncheon and a ski lodge-set b'nai mitzvah—two very different parties both held in The Ballroom. Depending on what tricks the designers have up their sleeves, the space can transform to fit practically any theme.

Photograph by Gregory Paul Photography

views

A venue isn't just a physical space in which to hold your event—it should be a place where you want to create memories. Go where somebody else can take the pressure off and allow you to fully enjoy yourself. You shouldn't have to worry about details during your event; know that the team you've chosen is going above and beyond to make the day magnificent.

AMEE FARM

COURTNEY DESENA | JOSEPH DESENA

Soon after Courtney and Joseph Desena bought Riverside Farm, a friend made the observation that if another property like theirs ever came up for sale, he would buy it immediately. A handful of years later, Amee Farm, a former whiskey distillery and one of the town's oldest properties, became available and the friend snatched it up. He mostly lives in New York City while the Desenas manage his property, which has now become one of the coziest and most charming places to stay and celebrate in New England.

Organic from the beginning, Amee Farm offers hosts the exceptional opportunity to serve their guests delicious homemade food that was most likely gathered that morning. The fresh, crisp linens and furnishings have an air of Martha Stewart about them, as if the DIY maven herself took a spin through the farmhouse before each event. The small town of Pittsfield, Vermont, happily welcomes out-of-town visitors giddy to celebrate a wedding, family reunion, or weekend getaway—indeed, after every event the town's lone bar is often bursting at the seams with overjoyed guests and locals alike.

Just as with Riverside Farm, Courtney and Joseph delight in customizing every special occasion to the wishes and whims of their hosts. Everything from a local wine and cheese tasting to an extravagant Indian wedding to an outdoor weekend adventure has taken place on the farms.

Roads used to be much narrower in this small town, so the first order of business was to move the house 500 feet back so that it sat on a scenic hill. While clearing the land, we discovered these enormous boulders that we incorporated into the landscaping and rock retaining wall. The natural pond only needed to be spruced up a bit.

Photograph by Courtney Desena

Photograph by Cronin Hill Photography

Photograph by Jen Curtis Photography

"It is entirely possible to be luxurious and rural at the same time."
—Courtney Desena

Right: Amee Farm's wraparound porch is the central gathering place. It's not unusual to see people curl up in an Adirondack chair with a blanket and a mug of hot apple cider and just gaze out over the valley. We overlook Killington and its ski resorts, so the view is nothing short of spectacular.

Facing page top: The privacy the farm affords is a tremendous benefit for many of our guests. When a group comes in for an event, they get to take over the entire farm—like having a bed-and-breakfast all to themselves. We're more than happy to arrange exciting activities, like outdoor barbeques or snowshoeing, but sometimes people are just happy to lounge and revel in each other's company.

Facing page bottom: We work in partnership with the local farmers to provide as many farm-to-table offerings as possible. Our food is upscale comfort food, hearty and homemade dishes that change with the seasons.

Photograph by Cronin Hill Photography

views

Don't ever let someone else tell you what your event should be like. If it has a factory-generated feel to it, your guests probably won't even remember it five years later. Use everything that is special about you as a guide to how your event should feel and look.

BEDFORD VILLAGE INN

JACK CARNEVALE

A fabulous bed-and-breakfast is often referred to as a region's best-kept secret, but with New Hampshire's Bedford Village Inn, the secret has been out for quite some time. NBC's Tom Brokaw called it "a place where you can eat very well and sleep very well," AAA has made it the state's longest-running recipient of the Four Diamond award, and the list of favorable reviews, honors, and claims to fame just keeps going and going. So it comes as no surprise that this sanctuary for rest, relaxation, unforgettable corporate meetings, and exquisite celebrations is a family-owned business. Bedford Village Inn is lovingly run by Jack Carnevale, his wife Andrea, son Jon, and 130 dedicated staff members who welcome guests—both regular patrons and first-time visitors—like old friends.

Beyond an elegant venue for events of all sorts, Bedford Village Inn is a permanent symbol of the townspeople's commitment to preserving a slice of American history. With records dating back to 1774, the property has had many lives: flax farm, birthplace of a couple's 14 children, home to a string of Shetland ponies, and now the site of an award-winning restaurant and inn. The restaurant is the reinvention of the 1810-built Federal-style farmhouse, and the luxurious guest suites and great hall are located within the original barn—now a well-appointed three-story haven for restoration and celebration surrounded by nearly six idyllic acres of greenery.

Our restaurant, sumptuous suites, elegant great hall, and other indoor spaces are enveloped by pristinely landscaped gardens that absolutely glow at night.

Photograph by John Gauvin, Studio One

Photograph by John Gauvin, Studio One

Photograph by John Gauvin, Studio One

Photograph by Tony Scarpetta, Scarpetta Photography

Photograph by Tony Scarpetta, Scarpetta Photography

"You know you've created a true destination when locals, as well as people who live a state away, choose it as a regular getaway and the place to host their most special occasions."
—Jack Carnevale

Indoors and out, the estate exudes a poetic romance; it nods to the town's rich heritage while offering all of the modern accoutrements that make life pleasurable. Our seasoned chef, expert sommelier, and helpful waitstaff—not to mention the fresh, gourmet cuisine and mouthwatering desserts—make dining a memorable experience. For the holidays, we invite interior and floral designers to express their creativity by giving each room its own theme, setting a festive atmosphere in keeping with the inn's natural sophistication and charm. Guests who wish to wander farther afield are surprised to find plenty of sights, museums, shops, and coastal adventures just a short drive from the oasis of Bedford.

Photograph by John Gauvin, Studio One

views

When selecting the location for your special event, be mindful of not only the property's location, looks, amenities, and staff, but also its reputation. Don't be bashful about asking for references, because the best venues will gladly share references for any type of event—social, corporate, or otherwise.

BOSTON HARBOR HOTEL

An architectural treasure situated at a historic waterfront setting, the Boston Harbor Hotel at Rowes Wharf sets the stage for any celebration. The venue is emblematic of the best of Boston: outside, the harbor and the city's most prestigious marina are steps away; inside, the luxurious décor is elegant, traditional, and most appropriate in a city that reveres its rich history. The Boston Harbor Hotel's most precious offering for any special event, however, is its staff. Celebrating here means being pampered by attendants who are thoughtful and gracious.

The city's only waterfront hotel, the Boston Harbor Hotel allows guests to experience a grand sense of arrival, whether they arrive by land or sea. Yachts and historic tall ships line Rowes Wharf. On the city side of the property, the hotel's front façade is accessorized by the dramatic cityscape of downtown Boston and the Rose Fitzgerald Kennedy Greenway, which weaves a ribbon of green stretching the length of the city.

Inside the hotel, a warm welcome awaits. The staff has developed a signature style of service that is genuine and considerate. Two ballrooms and multiple smaller spaces easily accommodate large corporate dinners, luxurious weddings, or intimate and joyous family gatherings. It's a setting where you can mark life's milestones with ceremony while creating magnificent memories that will last a lifetime.

A visit to the Boston Harbor Hotel leaves guests with no doubt that they are staying at a hotel that could only exist in Boston. Its architecture and design is distinctive to the city. With a copper-domed rotunda and dramatic archway that's referred to as the Gateway to the City of Boston, the building is one of the most photographed settings in New England.

Photograph by Kerry Brett

Photograph by Kerry Brett

"Selecting a unique venue is the starting point for creating the ultimate celebration."

—Paul J. Jacques

Right: As an independently owned hotel, we have had the opportunity to create our own signature style of service. Our staff has an immense sense of pride in everything we do. Every gesture we extend to our guests is genuine; nothing is generic about an experience here.

Facing page top: Our cuisine is extraordinary. Critically acclaimed Daniel Bruce has served as executive chef for more than two decades, ensuring that all guests experience inspiring flavors, creative pairings, and an artful presentation, whether they are dining in one of Bruce's three restaurants or at a special event. Indeed, the hotel's two signature events celebrate exceptional cuisine. Every winter we are defined by the three-month-long Boston Wine Festival, a food and wine pairing series that features world-class wine and complementary menus created by its founder, Chef Bruce. Every summer is celebrated with the Summer in the City entertainment series. Attendees can enjoy the waterfront while dining on the hotel's expansive terrace, listening to live bands, or watching classic films by moonlight. There is no better definition of summer in the city.

Facing page bottom: The Wharf and Atlantic rooms, our two ballrooms, embrace a traditional design while maintaining modern conveniences. The best feature of both ballrooms is the breathtaking view showcased by floor-to-ceiling windows on the water, a dazzling sight day or evening.

Photograph by Glenn Livermore Photography

views

We often meet couples whose greatest concern is pleasing their guests. Our piece of advice: let your guests be pleased by a celebration that best reflects you. Make every moment your own through signature accents that are self-expressive.

BOSTON OPERA HOUSE

JAMES JENSEN

Very few authentic vaudeville palaces remain in America, but even fewer exist as working theaters. The Boston Opera House is not only still in operation—it's now home to the Boston Ballet and numerous world-class and Broadway touring productions—it underwent a $50 million renovation in 2004 to restore what was originally known as the B. F. Keith Memorial Theatre to its original splendor.

Constructed in 1928 as a tribute to vaudeville's great impresario Benjamin Franklin Keith, the theater was a combination of preeminent architect Thomas White Lamb's extensive knowledge and an array of opulent materials. Imported carrara marble columns, real gold leaf details, sterling silver chandeliers, intricate filigree molding, elaborate plaster ceilings, and 100-percent silk tapestries still adorn the grand lobby and other more intimate rooms throughout the theater. With so many available event areas, the option to begin an event in one space before transitioning to another opens up a world of possibilities. Even the stage can set the scene for a dramatic dinner tableau in the spotlight.

Those who work at the Boston Opera House are experienced in orchestrating a flawless performance—it is, after all, what they do in the performing arts world every day. Production managers and event coordinators are on-hand to assist hosts with bringing their dream event to life. The historic building has welcomed weddings, bar and bat mitzvahs, corporate award shows, and even a fundraiser attended by the President of the United States, to name a few.

The luxury of the Boston Opera House was unrivaled in its time, and even today its stunning architecture and decoration elicits gasps from first-time visitors. While all of the mechanical, safety, and technological systems were updated during the renovation, the Old World craftsmanship was strictly maintained throughout the restoration of the building's décor. For example, when replicating the silk wall panels proved too large for modern looms, a loom was custom-built to create the historic pattern.

Photograph by Whitney Cox

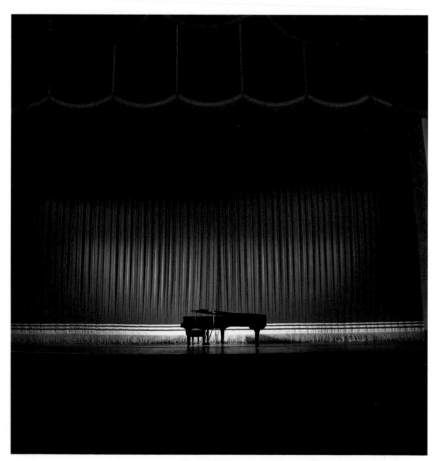

"Always keep in mind that you're renting more than just a space."
—James Jensen

The theater is a gem of a building; its unique aesthetics can enhance ideas and provide inspiration for all manner of celebrations. With seven different event spaces under one roof, guest lists that begin with 15 or top out at 2,500 can all find an appropriate setting.

Photograph by Greg Bolosky

views

Dealing primarily with large-scale performing arts companies has given us a valuable set of skills. Keeping track of timelines, coordinating sizeable groups of people, dealing with setup and take-down—these are remarkably similar to the talents required in the event world. At the end of the day, both are putting on a show.

THE BOSTON PUBLIC LIBRARY

To be in the presence of pages from the Gutenberg *Bible*, the ashes of Sacco and Vanzetti, and John Adams' personal library is simply inspiring. When that history is captured in a setting like the Boston Public Library, it's absolutely breathtaking.

Named by architect Charles Follen McKim as his "palace for the people," the Boston Public Library in Copley Square is an incredible sight, grandly seated in the heart of Back Bay. The Boston Public Library was founded in 1848 as the first large, free municipal library in the United States and was housed in a former schoolhouse on Mason Street and then a building on Boylston Street until McKim completed the present facility in Copley Square nearly 50 years later. In recent years, the library building has been revived to its original majesty, most recently with the historical McKim Building restoration and renovation.

In complete harmony with the stunning artifacts, books, and manuscripts held within its walls, the library boasts architecture full of spectacular statues, elegant marble, vaulted ceilings, and graceful arches. Among these fascinating surroundings, numerous event spaces exude a welcoming ambience, providing the versatility necessary to host small celebrations of 20 or large gatherings of 3,000. Guests feel embraced by the library's history and charm, which can only add to the style and personality of the event.

After passing through the low, broad entrance hall with its three aisles of heavy, Iowa sandstone piers—where vaulted ceilings offer names of famous Bostonians scribed into the marble mosaic—guests are greeted by the impressive main staircase. Ensconced in ivory grey marble that is mottled with fossil shells, the stairs are flanked by twin marble lions that are memorials to Massachusetts Second and Twentieth Civil War infantry regiments.

Photograph by Winslow Martin

"A deep history, whether it's your own or the location's, makes everything seem more meaningful."
—Emily Tenney

Top right: The main staircase leads up to the Puvis de Chavannes Gallery, which is named after the French artist whose mural paintings adorn the space.

Bottom right: The charming interior courtyard, centered around the bronze cast fountain statue, is the perfect atmosphere for a private celebration.

Facing page top: The McKim Building's classic serenity is showcased by the first impression of the façade as well as in the details—such as the inscriptions underneath the windows and the medallions in the spandrels of the window arches.

Facing page bottom left: Special lighting transforms the sumptuous Abbey Room, which features *The Quest of the Holy Grail* murals and a remarkable ornamented ceiling, into a lively party space.

Facing page bottom right: Named after the library's first great benefactor, Bates Hall is a majestic reading room that remains one of the most historically significant spaces of this national historic landmark.

Photograph by Sean W. Hennessy

views

The generic event just isn't popular anymore. Look for locations and elements that will add a bit of pizzazz to the event without compromising the style and personality desired. Brainstorm with friends, browse magazines, and speak with many professionals to find ideas that really fit with the vision and purpose for the celebration.

THE BUSHNELL CENTER
FOR THE PERFORMING ARTS

CATHERINE STEPHENS

To know that your guests are mingling on the same stage once graced by legendary actress and Connecticut native Katharine Hepburn is an extraordinary feeling. It becomes even more fantastic when the names Jolson, Chaplin, Toscanini, Bernstein, Perlman, Pavarotti, Olivier, Garland, Brando, and Baryshnikov are added to the list of performers who once trod the boards. After serving as the setting for an impressive eight decades of cultural history, The Bushnell Center for the Performing Arts offers an event experience unlike any other venue.

Dotha Bushnell Hillyer opened The Horace Bushnell Memorial Hall on January 13, 1930 as a "living memorial" to her father, an esteemed Hartford minister, theologian, philosopher, and civic leader. The traditional Georgian exterior and rich Art Deco interior were designed by the renowned architectural firm of Corbett, Harrison and MacMurray, who would later use The Bushnell as a prototype for their next big venture, Radio City Music Hall. In 2001, a 90,000-square-foot facility that includes the Maxwell M. and Ruth R. Belding Theater was built adjacent to what is now known as Mortensen Hall. These buildings combined constitute The Bushnell Center, the site of touring Broadway productions, orchestral concerts, charity benefits, and even the 1996 presidential debate between Bill Clinton and Bob Dole.

With so many marvelous artistic tales swirling about the place, it's practically impossible to host a wedding, anniversary party, corporate gathering, or birthday bash without feeling like entertainment royalty.

The courtyard between the Mortensen and the Belding Theaters is an excellent setting to begin an evening's drama. We've been known to roll out the red carpet for arriving guests, and hosts can even design custom "show posters" to be displayed outside of the theater. Seasonal landscaping and trees lit with hundreds of twinkle lights during the holidays further enhance the magic.

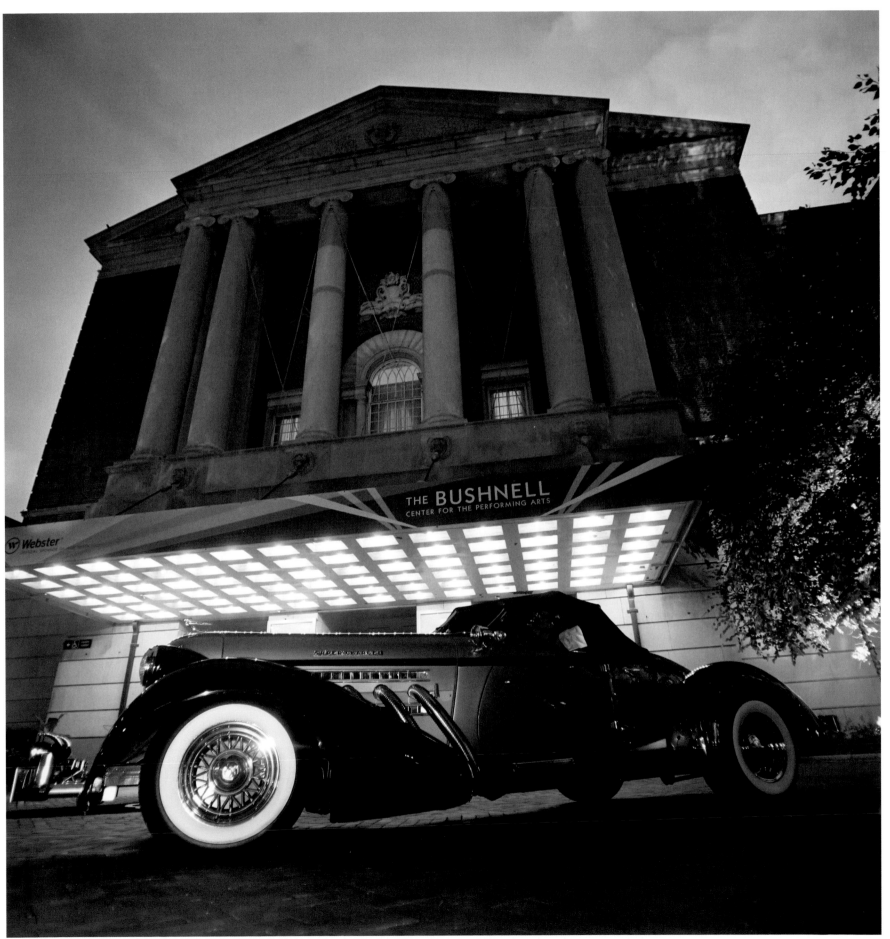

"For those few hours, your guests are the stars of the show."

—Catherine Stephens

Right: The Autorino Great Hall is a truly dramatic space completely enclosed in glass. The gable-vaulted ceiling rises 35 feet above the floor and provides the backdrop for a unique glass chandelier designed by Dale Chihuly. Known as the gem of the theater, Chihuly's *Ode to Joy* often appears to be floating in mid-air.

Facing page: We have a variety of spaces suitable for many different types of events, from intimate suites to grand lobbies to even the stages themselves. For example, we'll have a wedding ceremony onstage at the Mortensen or Belding and then have the guests move to the lobby for cocktails. When they return, the curtain will rise dramatically on the breathtaking sight of their reception. Our sound, lighting, and projection specialists are theatrical union members, so it is entirely possible to create even the most fanciful worlds. Max Catering, our exclusive in-house caterer and part of the Max Restaurant Group, presents an unmatched versatile approach to gourmet cuisine and expert service.

Photograph by Robert Benson Photography

views

Having a memorable event starts with a unique location. Rather than transforming a space entirely, choosing a venue that's already imbued with a sense of history can elevate any gathering to a truly remarkable event.

CASTLE HILL INN

The story of Castle Hill is older than the United States of America, reaching back to 1740, when England declared war against Spain and erected a watch house that was replaced by a summer house in 1874 for renowned scientist and explorer Alexander Agassiz, whose oceanographic expeditions formed the basis for the modern science of marine biology. And while history is a great appeal, the scenic 40-acre peninsula as well as the staff's dedication to food and service keep guests coming back.

For more than a century, the pristine enclave hosting the inn and lighthouse has been a Newport landmark, and the guest quarters at Castle Hill retain the warmth and quiet luxury of 19th-century seacoast life. Castle Hill offers a relaxed yet lofty, comfortable atmosphere amidst exquisite natural surroundings, making it a popular and elegant location for weddings. Every single event is customized and geared toward a couple's background, making each different and memorable in its own way. It is the personal touches and the food—the organic cooking, the produce and seafood sourced from local farmers and fishermen—that illustrate Castle Hill's dedication to quality and heritage.

Overlooking Newport Harbor and Narragansett Bay, the inn stands at the end of a tree-lined driveway flanked by beach houses and cottages. The inn presents guests with a spectacular view upon approach.

Photograph by Warren Jagger

Photograph by Warren Jagger

Photograph by Warren Jagger

Photograph by Stoneblossoms

Newport Harbor and Narragansett Bay backdrop the Chalet Terrace and surrounding green space while framing a breathtaking view from inside the inn. Both traditional and contemporary event designs are complemented by the historical property, and the casually elegant spaces are perfect for a small, intimate party, a black tie affair, or a clambake reception. Our culinary team artfully crafts fresh local fish, regional meats, and produce into distinctly native, seasonal menus. One of our scallop dishes speaks volumes about the food and the time spent in putting together each entrée.

Photograph by Angel Tucker

views

It is important to plan early and spend time on the details. Surround your event with designers and vendors who understand your vision and are familiar with the property.

FOUR SEASONS HOTEL BOSTON

Located in the heart of Back Bay and facing the beautiful Boston Public Garden, America's first public botanical garden, Four Seasons Hotel Boston plays host to family celebrations, corporate galas, weddings, and everything in between. All are creatively designed to match the host's personal tastes and then flawlessly executed by the hotel's team of experienced event professionals.

New England's only five-star, five-diamond property, the hotel enjoys close proximity to countless cultural, historic, and outdoor attractions, which makes weekend getaways all the more memorable and invigorating. Fenway Park, Newbury Street, the theater district, the Freedom Trail—a walking or trolley tour of 16 historic sites—and the Charles River Esplanade, plus dozens of other must-see destinations, are just a few minutes away.

In addition to its supreme location, the hotel is well-known for its award-winning service and stylish décor. Events too are renowned for serving mouthwatering, customized, and beautifully presented cuisine such as hand-rolled pastas, steaks cooked to perfection, and the freshest New England seafood. Guests interested in continuing the festivities the day after a special event are invited to stroll the gardens and nearby quaint streets of Beacon Hill, or to enjoy afternoon tea and live music performed nightly in the hotel's Bristol Lounge restaurant, heralded as "Boston's living room."

The stunning florals embody the feel of a memorable evening event in the Grand Ballroom—the largest of the event spaces. This majestic room overlooks the Boston Public Garden and boasts all the latest high-tech and audiovisual offerings.

"Working with a team that is brimming with creativity, talent, and passion allows the hosts to take their event to the next level."

—Jim Peters

The hotel offers many diverse function settings which serve as exciting alternatives to the Grand Ballroom. These include a unique, curved room featuring an Italian glass chandelier and windows that span the length of the room. During a reception, New England-inspired small plates such as the trio of salmon or lobster three ways provide a unique flair. Executive chef Brooke Vosika customizes menus for each host using the freshest local ingredients.

Photograph by Claudia Kronenberg

views

To ensure that every event is unforgettable, collaboration and communication between the host and hotel staff are essential. These elements will create an event that is unique, exciting, authentic, and flawless from start to finish.

GEDNEY FARM AND MEPAL MANOR

MICHAEL SMITH

To city dwellers, there's nothing more enticing than a jaunt to rustic country grounds for a refreshing change of pace. The lure of historic lodgings with all the modern amenities can prove irresistible. Urbanites find themselves regularly drawn to the twin inns of Gedney Farm and Mepal Manor, which provide all that and a polished event space and fully furnished spa facility.

In the early 1900s, New Marlborough, Massachusetts, was populated by affluent families from New York developing business ventures on their country real estate. The Willets family founded Gedney Farm for dairy and the breeding of Percheron stallions, and—on the other end of the village a mile away—the Bloodgood family raised Hackney ponies and cocker spaniels at Mepal Farm. In the mid-1980s, Bradford Wagstaff and Leslie Miller converted the Gedney dairy barn into a 16-room guesthouse. They eventually renovated the property's former horse barn into a special event venue and acquired the Mepal Farm property. The renamed Mepal Manor opened in 2001 after a thorough restoration as a 12-room hotel and spa.

Both the farm and the manor grew in tandem, and great care was taken to ensure that the buildings' reuse would positively impact the architectural integrity of the original structures. Each room is beautifully appointed, and the manors are well sited amidst open green spaces and the village's lovely period homes. The two venues feature professional full kitchens with completely customizable menus. And with guests hailing from New York and other urban centers in mind, the stunningly designed Mepal Spa features four treatment rooms, a salon, a yoga and movement space, a quiet room, and a hot tub. Faithful yet innovative, Mepal Manor and Gedney Farm provide the ideal location for guests seeking a unique, classic destination for a getaway or an event.

Although the two properties are different visually, they share the underlying concept of preserving, utilizing, and adapting existing historic spaces. Hospitality and farming do, after all, go hand in hand. At Mepal Manor, the largely covered terrace offers completely private, unspoiled views of receding tree-covered hills and meadows. 150 acres of open pasture offer a ready location for grazing cattle.

Photograph by Eric Limón

Photograph by Eric Limón

Photograph by Eric Limón

Photograph courtesy of Gedney Farm and Mepal Manor

"The very roots of New England's rich history are beautiful architecture, an agricultural lifestyle, and wholesome and delicious food."

—Michael Smith

Style is a key element in what we do. The Gedney Farm horse barn was renovated to create three separate levels, including a loft space, and is capable of hosting up to 250 for fine dining events. During special events, horse-drawn carriages may ferry guests of honor to and from the manor and the farm, and Gedney Farm's event and lodging buildings are nestled close together, separated by a cozy courtyard.

Photograph courtesy of Gedney Farm and Mepal Manor

views

Our venues and amenities developed organically from the various requests and suggestions we received over the years. Truly listening to what our guests have to say is the best thing we can do as managers and we work hard to ensure that everyone leaves fully satisfied.

THE INSTITUTE OF CONTEMPORARY ART

GREGG FONTECCHIO

Distinguished as one of the country's earliest museums dedicated to contemporary art, The Institute of Contemporary Art comprises four fabulous venues within one artful building. State Street Corporation Lobby is a dramatic space with floor-to-ceiling glass and views of downtown Boston; Water Café and its adjacent patio are perfect for intimate parties; Putnam Investments Plaza is a wholly outdoor venue that can easily be tented as the weather requires; and Barbara Lee Family Foundation Theater has the unique flexibility of going from total blackout to softly lit with sheer draperies to uninterrupted sightlines of Boston Harbor. Whether welcoming the general public or an event host's special guests, the institute and its art are truly transformative.

Designed by legendary firm Diller Scofidio + Renfro, the architecture echoes the forward-minded philosophies of the artists whose work is so beautifully displayed. The ICA lays claim to introducing Americans to what are now household names like Georges Braque, Edvard Munch, Andy Warhol, and Roy Lichtenstein. The tradition continues today with the leadership's commitment to supporting emerging artists—experts in paint, printing, film, video, media, performance, and literature.

The trendsetting ICA naturally makes a fabulous venue for events avant-garde and elegant alike, especially with the culinary masterminds of Wolfgang Puck Catering on-site to serve up their signature fresh, innovative, palate-pleasing fare. From simple cocktail parties to formal seated dinners, there's hardly an event that wouldn't be all the more grand in the ICA's art-infused setting.

The annual wine dinner and auction held in the theater is a tremendously important fundraising opportunity for the museum. While enjoying signature cuisine, perfectly paired wines, and stunning views of the water, 180 invited guests gather in support of the arts. The event would not be possible without the support of industry peers like PBD Events, Winston Flowers, and Be Our Guest.

Photograph by Dave Robbins

Photograph by Dave Robbins

Photograph by Dave Robbins

Photograph by Liz Linder

"The best event venue has the potential to take on any ambience, evoke any period of time."
—Gregg Fontecchio

An impressive crowd of 700 attended club night with artist Shepard Fairey—more than 20 of his screen prints are part of our permanent collection. Though art events are a natural fit for the museum, it is really quite conducive to occasions of all sorts.

views

Before you choose a venue, you need to carefully consider what elements of the event you value most, if you want to have the entire program at one site, and what kind of experience and memories you want to create. Answering these questions will help you determine how formal or casual of an event is right for you. From there, bring in the experts who will make the day seamless.

ISABELLA STEWART GARDNER MUSEUM

PETER CROWLEY

Who wouldn't have wanted to be on Isabella Gardner's VIP list at the turn of the 20th century? She hosted exclusive soirées for Boston's high society with celebrity guests from the realms of fine art, literature, and music. As a respected patron of the arts, world traveler, and collector of paintings and sculpture from every corner of the globe, Isabella had a vision of showcasing her unparalleled collection in a unique museum dedicated to the "education and enjoyment of the public forever."

Inspired by the grand palazzo of Venice, the Isabella Stewart Gardner Museum was designed to reflect classical Italian architecture with manicured gardens and an enclosed courtyard flooded with natural light. The beloved museum remains as it was conceived in 1903: an artistic, musical, and horticultural landmark honoring innovation and scholarly thinking. Isabella was not bound by convention and enjoyed welcoming freethinkers to her palazzo. Today the beautiful property, an intimate setting for hosting special events, is home to original art galleries, a concert and lecture hall, and a charming café. Further expansion features a new wing designed by Pritzker Prize-winning architect Renzo Piano. This stunning new space houses an exhibition gallery to showcase select works from the permanent collection as well as changing exhibitions of contemporary art. The Gardner has rich historic value, yet possesses a fresh, vibrant ambience even after 100 years. Today's social, nonprofit, and corporate celebrations fit perfectly.

We creatively transformed Fenway Court from a flowering display by day into a glowing palazzo by night, with softly illuminated garden statuary and pastel stucco walls. Gatherings in the cloisters are reminiscent of Isabella's own gracious entertaining style.

"A special occasion is truly eventful when held in a magical place with a deep sense of history."
—Peter Crowley

Right: Caramelized sea scallops and asparagus drizzled with miso hazelnut vinaigrette has a decidedly Asian twist, reflecting Isabella's fascination with the Far East. There, she collected many treasures that are part of the museum's permanent collection.

Facing page top left: Rack of lamb with porcini and barolo jus express the bold flavors of the autumn season.

Facing page top right and bottom left: Chrysanthemums in the Courtyard is a renowned garden display featuring dramatic kiku grown in the single-stem ogiku style. Vivid flowering vines up to 20 feet long cascade from balconies at the annual Hanging Nasturtiums installation, a springtime tradition begun by Isabella a century ago. Vibrant plant life blooms year-round amid ancient sculptures, honoring the founder's horticultural legacy.

Facing page bottom right: An elegant riff on the traditional Provençal fish stew, New England bouillabaisse pays tribute to the sea's bounty. Whether we are expecting 100 dinner guests or planning a standing reception for 250 with passed hors d'oeuvres, chef Peter Crowley can tailor the menu and wine list to the host's individual taste.

Photograph by Cheryl Richards

views

Exclusive art museum settings are in demand and private events are usually limited to a few evenings per month, so it's best to plan ahead. Guided gallery tours can be arranged for guests. Whether you choose a chamber ensemble, vocalists, or a jazz trio, the property is equipped for musical entertainment as well as seamless audio-visual presentations.

THE LIBERTY HOTEL

CHRISTINA CHUNIAS

The Liberty Hotel—an adaptive reuse project and architectural gem—overlooks the Charles River and its esplanade and sits at the foot of Beacon Hill. The national historic landmark is cruciform in shape and has been a prominent structure in Boston since 1851, and from then until 1990 the edifice served as The Charles Street Jail. Ideally located, the luxury hotel offers easy access to the Boston Common, TD Garden, shopping, the financial district, and the regal Longfellow Bridge leading into Cambridge.

The Liberty Hotel, open since 2007, is where the past and the present meet. Due to meticulous planning reflective of the property's colorful past, guests can marvel at the vestiges of jail cells within the hotel's restaurant, bar, and historic gallery. A sophisticated contemporary interior décor integrates with the architecture's beautiful simplicity and exterior of Quincy granite while American Colonial prints—enlarged and rendered in historic colors such as maroon, grey, and purple—provide a fresh take on a traditional look.

A mainstay of the city for more than a century, the hotel provides the quintessential Boston experience. The venue offers more than 6,000 square feet of function space, including the use of the catwalks within the structure's expansive 90-foot rotunda. The building is home to a multitude of public spaces—including lobby and reception areas, two restaurants, two bars, and outdoor patio space for drinking and dining. An adjoining 16-story tower houses the majority of the 298 guestrooms, which are equipped with every modern convenience. The staff provides the highest level of service, proving The Liberty Hotel to be an elegant venue of the loftiest stature.

The stately, modern entryway artfully contrasts the rough texture of Quincy granite, brought in by railcar in the mid-1800s. Reproductions of the originals, the large windows bathe the lobby and function rooms in natural light. In the evening, accent lighting warms the space. The bars to the left of the entryway on the property's west wing were reinstalled during the project and nod to the building's historical prominence.

Photograph by Brian Phillips

Photograph by Toby Lawrence

Photograph by Michael Wechsler

"A luxury hotel that reflects the place, history, and energy of its city will always afford the most unique and unforgettable experiences."
—Rachel Moniz

Whether for a corporate event, wedding, or a casual lounge atmosphere, The Liberty Hotel provides a variety of unique function rooms, each lit differently to bring out distinct personalities. All function rooms are equipped with drop projectors and screens and Bose sound. The Liberty Ballroom, in addition to the inherent equipment, is also outfitted with a "smart" podium to afford control of the lights, blinds, and all embedded technology. The 3,000-square-foot Liberty Ballroom represents half of the hotel's functional space. Its chandeliers and décor—designed by Alexandra Champalimaud—are period in design, and the carpet is patterned after stained glass in Beacon Hill. In the rotunda, up-lit tapestries bearing oak trees bring life into the space and frame the cellblock's previous location. The vastness of the space allows for private parties for as many as 800 people.

Photograph by Person + Killian Photography

views

When trying to decide on a venue, remember to consider the character appropriate to the occasion. Place is one of the most important elements in forging a specific atmosphere, and the proper space will give any event wings.

MUSEUM OF FINE ARTS, BOSTON

GREGG FONTECCHIO

Home to some of the rarest and most important artistic treasures in the world, the Museum of Fine Arts, Boston offers something for everyone. Each year, approximately one million people walk through the doors of the MFA to explore objects ranging from ancient Egyptian mummies to contemporary photography. The encyclopedic collection creates a perfect backdrop to host a wide-range of events. When visitors depart for the evening, the space can be transformed to meet an array of private soirée needs, providing an opportunity for invited guests to experience the art and the architecture on a more intimate level.

Since opening its doors on Huntington Avenue in 1909, the MFA has undergone many architectural changes. Fall 2010 marked the completion of a major expansion and renovation project by the internationally renowned firm Foster + Partners. The project resulted in renovated galleries, a new wing for the Art of the Americas, and the dramatic glass-enclosed Ruth and Carl J. Shapiro Family Courtyard. These new and newly revitalized spaces enhance the museum's entertaining experience.

Second only to the art and its beautiful surroundings are the delectable culinary offerings dreamed up for each special occasion by the museum's exclusive caterer, Restaurant Associates. Having catered casual and formal events of all sizes and for all audiences—private, corporate, and charity—Restaurant Associates ensures that guests will long remember the artistically prepared fare: refreshing appetizers, specialty drinks, gourmet main courses, and mouthwatering desserts.

In 1916, the museum invited beloved American artist John Singer Sargent to create murals for the rotunda. Sargent provided multiple paintings and sculptures and reconfigured the space to unite architecture, painting, and sculpture into a harmonious display evocative of the museum's exquisite collections.

Right and facing page top: From the Huntington Avenue entrance on the Avenue of the Arts to the numerous galleries and public spaces, a sense of history and grandeur pervades the museum.

Facing page bottom: Designed in the spirit of a European palace, the William I. Koch Gallery showcases European paintings from 1550-1700, including masterpieces by El Greco, Rubens, and Velázquez. Clad in travertine stone and measuring 100 feet in length, the space accommodates up to 230 seated guests or 700 guests for a cocktail-style reception. In contrast to the Koch Gallery's classical ambience, the Shapiro Family Courtyard is larger—seating up to 400—and decidedly more contemporary. Designed by Foster + Partners, the spectacular glass enclosed courtyard features year-round views of the outdoors in an architecturally stunning space.

Photograph © Museum of Fine Arts, Boston

views

The museum's collection is made up of Art of the Americas; Art of Europe; Contemporary Art; Art of Asia, Oceania, and Africa; Art of the Ancient World; Prints, Drawings, and Photographs; Textile and Fashion Arts; and Musical Instruments. Because of this diversity, both art enthusiasts and newcomers to the world of art can find plenty of cultural inspiration in a place of learning, exploration, and celebration.

NEW BRITAIN MUSEUM OF AMERICAN ART

DOUGLAS HYLAND

Walls of glass greet visitors to the New Britain Museum of American Art, framing a quietly beautiful view of the rolling hills and ancient oak trees of Walnut Hill Park. Designed by Frederick Law Olmsted, the landscape architect behind the beloved Central Park, Walnut Hill Park plays neighbor to the museum, gifting the typically enclosed atmosphere of an art gallery with an unexpected vision of breathtaking nature. Playing against type is something the museum knows well: what began as an industrialist's personal mansion has expanded since its official 1937 public opening into a fusion of the old and new, with all spaces dedicated to showcasing more than 10,000 paintings, sculpture, drawings, photographs, and illustrations depicting the journey of American life. The "new" came in 2006, when Ann Beha Architects completed an addition of 13 new galleries and four public spaces that critics hailed as a transparent temple of art that mixes New York ambience with Yankee ingenuity and all-American beauty.

The roomy Stanley Works Center presents an elegant blank slate for events of any theme. The adjoining Café on the Park can convert to a dance floor, its terrace providing direct access to the outdoors. Adjacent galleries are perfect for cocktails and hors d'oeuvres, with guests encouraged to stroll freely throughout the entire museum. Having been the setting for events ranging from early morning corporate breakfasts to sophisticated evening weddings, the New Britain Museum presents its visitors with more than simply a space to gather. Artistic representations of everything from the Colonial pioneers and founding fathers to 9/11 add a unique, educational layer to every festivity and make for great conversation starters.

Acknowledged as the first museum in the world dedicated solely to collecting and exhibiting American art, the New Britain Museum is renowned for its preeminent collection spanning three centuries of American artistic output. With the opening in 2006 of the Chase Family Building, the museum gave the collection a home it deserves.

Photograph by Victoria Souza Photography

Photograph by Carla Ten Eyck Photography

Photograph by Lorraine Greenfield Photography

Photograph by H. Robert Thiesfield

"The world of art is also the world of conversation, observation, and discussion."

—Douglas Hyland

Right: Powerful large-scale images are a dramatic setting for any event held in the contemporary gallery. Graydon Parrish's *The Cycle of Terror and Tragedy, September 11, 2001* is one of many not-to-be-missed gems of the New Britain Museum's collection, which also includes Dale Chihuly's spectacular *Blue and Beyond Blue* glass chandelier, Thomas Hart Benton's mural cycle *The Arts of Life in America*, and the 23 artist-designed benches—art you can sit on—that are sprinkled throughout the facility.

Facing page top left: Artist Mundy Hepburn's whimsical, luminous, electrified glass sculptures in *Joyous Windows* provide a kaleidoscope of swirling patterns and multicolored light that sets the mood for special celebrations

Facing page top right: The on-site presence of JORDAN Caterers.Design.Event Planners makes for a perfect marriage with the fine art and architecture of the museum. Consistent "best of" winners, the staff at JORDAN takes pride in executing customized, one-of-a-kind events that produce incredible memories.

Facing page bottom left: The rich cherry walls of the 2,322-square-foot Stanley Works Center for Education and Community Development and floor-to-ceiling windows overlooking Walnut Hill Park provide the perfect backdrop for corporate entertaining, social celebrations, milestone events, and elegant weddings.

Facing page bottom right: The museum's slogan "Where Art Meets Life" is exemplified by the special experience of dining amongst the art. The orangutans in Walton Ford's *Fallen Mias* seem to be part of The ART Party of the Year, the museum's spring gala and auction. Upward of 400 arts supporters gather each year for a lively, black-tie evening of bidding, dining, and dancing.

views

Museums have always been social institutions, sparking conversations and promoting personal reflection in people of all ages, nationalities, and beliefs. Every year we welcome visitors from across the U.S. and all over the world, demonstrating that art is universal. What better way to break the ice with a new acquaintance than to discuss a provocative painting or unusual sculpture? Providing your guests with something neutral to the party that they can all interpret and appreciate can launch any number of new relationships.

PEABODY ESSEX MUSEUM

NATALIA LASKARIS

Any event designer will tell you that the key to a truly memorable event is creating the perfect ambience, and there's quite possibly no better ambience than Salem's Peabody Essex Museum. Located in one of the most historically significant towns in the country, the museum has its roots in Salem's global maritime trade of the late 18th and early 19th centuries. Today the museum is home to over a million artworks from around the world. And this culturally rich, architecturally stunning place hosts events large and small, contemporary and traditional—each promising a transformative experience.

From its three-story, glass-ceilinged atrium to its numerous galleries and its rare-book library, the museum offers a variety of entertainment spaces. A talented team of event planning professionals is on location to help facilitate every aspect of the design and execution, making the process simple and enjoyable. With painstaking attention to detail, PEM staff members ensure that each guest has an enriching and engaging experience, one that will live on in story and memory. The Peabody Essex Museum's history helps others create their own.

The soaring, three-story atrium provides a dramatic space for large events. Its neutral palette and expansive glass ceiling afford a great deal of design latitude, allowing us to bring any theme to life.

"A great venue has the power to affect guests on an emotional level."
—Natalia Laskaris

One of the first museums in America to display works of art and culture from around the world, the museum lays claim to some of the most significant Asian, African, Oceanic, and maritime collections in existence. Our gallery spaces allow guests to dine and mingle among these precious objects. From the original East India Marine Hall's arched, floor-to-ceiling windows to the Bartlett and Copeland galleries' display cases of Chinese porcelain and the Phillips Library Reading Room's gold-leafed cornices, history radiates from every corner of our intimate spaces. We have just the right setting for any event, whether it's an afternoon luncheon for 20 or a business meeting for several hundred.

Photograph by Person + Killian Photography

views

❖ Hire professionals to plan and execute your event. This will help ensure an anxiety-free experience.

❖ If you plan to host out-of-town guests at your event, choose a venue that's centrally located and close to area attractions.

❖ The vision should come from you. The right entertainment space will help bring your vision to life.

RIVERSIDE FARM

COURTNEY DESENA | JOSEPH DESENA

Courtney and Joseph Desena were living in New York City when the Twin Towers fell, and it was that tragic event that spurred them into turning their dream of living on a farm into a reality. On a scouting flight to Jackson Hole, Wyoming, they discovered a real estate brochure left behind on their seat. Inside was a listing for a bucolic farmhouse in a quaint Vermont town; within a matter of days it was theirs. After undertaking an extensive renovation and hosting their own wedding in the barn, the Desenas started receiving unexpected visitors, people inquiring if the farm was a B&B or if it was available for weddings and receptions. Courtney and Joseph followed fate's suggestion and in 2004, on their one-year anniversary, they hosted their first professional wedding at Riverside Farm.

Perched on a hill with a spectacular view of the valley, Riverside Farm is in an idyllic location that immediately brings to mind Norman Rockwell paintings, brilliant fall foliage, and the scent of fresh-baked cookies. Guest cottages dot the 300-plus acres, and it's not uncommon for a group of outdoorsy guests to take to the hiking, biking, and horseback trails before donning their formal duds. Since entertaining comes naturally to the Desenas, it seemed like an obvious choice to open their home and land to people looking for an unpretentious, private, and picturesque place to celebrate.

Stonewell Barn is the largest of our three fully restored post-and-beam barns on the property. It's both air-conditioned and heated, so it's a comfortable venue whether the flowers are blooming or the snowflakes are swirling.

Photograph by Cronin Hill Photography

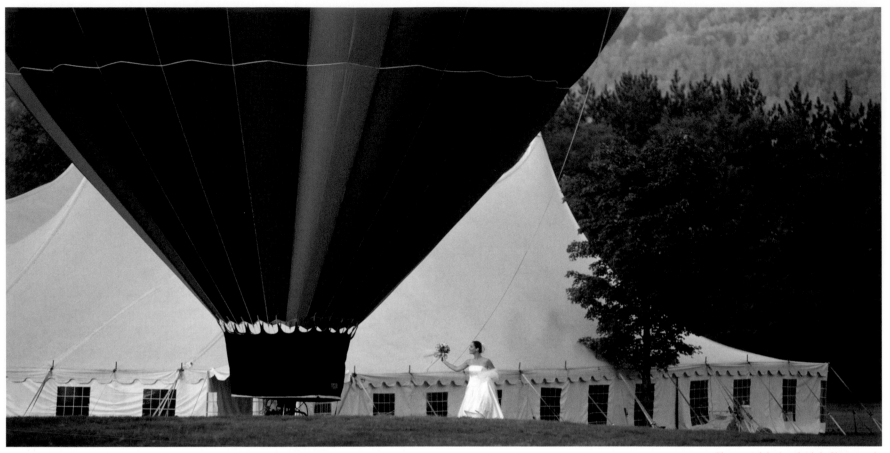

"Sometimes it takes getting away from the noise of the city to make people realize that friends and family are more important than all the traditional wedding bells and whistles that can accompany a luxurious wedding."

—Courtney Desena

Right: We love showing the best elements of Vermont to our guests. Everything about this place is warm and genuine, and that attitude can become infectious.

Facing page top: There are about 50 acres of just open meadow on the property, enough to accommodate a 450-person wedding—and a hot air balloon!

Facing page bottom left: All the renovations on Riverside Farm were done using materials reclaimed from the property. The covered bridge where guests enter Stonewell Barn provides a fantastic view of both the main area below and the architectural beams above. A copper-plated bar is installed at one end, adding a hip yet still pastoral touch to the room.

Facing page bottom right: Michele Mottola Special Events Consulting planned an absolutely lovely wedding for Marc Hall of Winston Flowers in Boston. The juxtaposition of the massive glass chandeliers with the delicate blooms and rural wooden surroundings was striking.

Photograph by Cronin Hill Photography

views

Planning an event can be extremely stressful, so having the opportunity to escape from the real world for a few days and concentrate solely on the important people in your life is invaluable. Coming to an almost isolated place like Pittsfield, Vermont, allows people to unplug from their busy lives and just enjoy themselves.

Photograph by Keller + Keller

Photograph by Claudia Kronenberg

Photograph courtesy of the White Elephant

"Nantucket feels like you've stepped back in time."

—Bettina Landt

Charm and elegance exude from every room and square inch of space, from the sculpture of Trunket, the mascot, to the hotel's magnificent harborfront presence. Guests can indulge in Nantucket's fresh seafood, such as seared bluefin tuna, and end a perfect summer day overlooking the harbor. We can accommodate most events, whether indoors on our heated awning-covered deck or outside with the natural watercolor hues of sea and sky blending exquisitely with the occasion.

views

Training, planning, training, planning. That's what keeps us running smoothly. For our staff, we look for attitude, overall friendly demeanor, and natural skill of pleasing people. We feel that everything else can be taught.

SUZANNE B. LOWELL LIGHTING DESIGN, INC.
SUZANNE B. LOWELL

Suzanne B. Lowell has been expertly illuminating incredible moments for the majority of her life, but it took a change of platform to inspire her to form her own company. A lighting designer for theatrical and dance productions by training, Suzanne discovered the many similarities between stage and event lighting when a friend asked her to design a party 15 years ago. Since that time, Suzanne has been applying her stage technique to social events.

No matter the medium, lighting design relies heavily upon collaboration, a practice that Suzanne has always considered the key factor in any successful event. Event lighting must truly support all of the visual elements relative to the celebration. The effect that color, pattern, and even the angle of light have on linens, floral work, and people is significant. That approach, learned from her years in the theater, has allowed Suzanne and her team to work with some of the best event professionals in the business.

Working closely with her hosts is another integral part of creating the perfect lighting design. Suzanne discovers what people are drawn toward, even if they think that it has nothing to do with the event that they are planning. By truly connecting with people, Suzanne is better able to create flattering and effective designs.

Pairing crisp, contemporary spotlights with classic crystal chandeliers was considered avant-garde only a few years ago. Watching the bride glide in and out of pools of light, guests were treated to a surreal, dreamlike effect for the ceremony. Event design by Hopple Popple; floral design by Domenic Cambio.

Photograph by Earl Christie

Photograph by Earl Christie   *Photograph by Earl Christie*   *Photograph by Brian Phillips Photography*

Above: Lighting helps to better define floral color and texture. Pin spots can visually separate petals, cast light through more delicate blooms, and create a halo effect upon lighter-colored blossoms. Events planned by Michele Mottola, Lynn Enos, and The Simple Details; floral design by Marc Hall of Winston Flowers and William Mizuta Private Florist.

Facing page: Layering and reflecting light is an interesting way of creating greater visual depth. Rich color hues bounce off the acrylic, glass, and mirrored surfaces, making the tables—and room—sparkle. Feathered white top lighting cuts through the ambient light and nicely defines the floral work and table appointments. Event planning by Michele Mottola Special Events Consulting; floral design by Marc Hall of Winston Flowers.

Previous pages: The continued use of white pools of light suggested a visual continuity throughout the guest areas. Event design by Hopple Popple; floral design by Domenic Cambio.

"Certain colors make you look at things more readily; they grab your eye and draw it up."
—Suzanne B. Lowell

"The key to powerful lighting design is choosing your focal points and making sure they're showcased properly."

—Suzanne B. Lowell

Right and facing page: Fire was the first organic, portable source of light. There is something so sexy and alluring about its heat and power. Flickering fire pits are a rustic and elegant addition to a snowy Vermont wedding—even the scent of burning wood is sensory. Event planning by Michele Mottola Special Events Consulting; floral design by Marc Hall of Winston Flowers.

Previous pages: Background color can dramatically affect the way in which a room is perceived. Changing just the shade of the ceiling can suggest some form of transition. Event planning by Michele Mottola Special Events Consulting; floral design by Marc Hall of Winston Flowers.

views

Lighting is as much of a design element as anything else. Sources of light, such as candlelight, architectural fixtures, and daylight have a considerable effect on the overall atmosphere. Knowing what other light might be present in the space helps the lighting designer form the best plan.

BE OUR GUEST

SIMONE WILLIAMSON

Since 1986, Be Our Guest has taken party rentals to an entirely new level. Discarding the old way of doing things, president Simone Williamson and her team have transformed the company into a highly specialized boutique that can accommodate nearly any style or project.

Focusing first on the treatment of its patrons, Simone has organized a dedicated staff that can swell to 130 members when needed. Passionate about events, many staff members have long been involved in the catering industry, so they understand the inner workings of an event and are proactive about what needs to be done. Every member, from the delivery drivers—who are called ambassadors because of their close interaction with the event host—to the receptionist and the designers, embodies careful attention to detail and a stellar collaborative attitude.

Equally as important as the people, Be Our Guest's rental products are acquired and maintained with an unprecedented level of consideration. Unbelievably selective, Simone chooses nothing but the best equipment and décor, only offering what she herself would be proud to use at her own event. Both traditional and custom items, like linens by the fabulous in-house fabric designer or china crafted specifically for Be Our Guest, are housed in a 2,200-square-foot showroom, where interested parties can browse the selections and play with various combinations. Whichever pieces are ultimately selected, there will be no question about the quality and the service that accompanies them.

A magnificent dinner overlooking Maine's pristine Prouts Neck bay area was enhanced with our green gazebo etched glassware that was selected by Churchill Catered Events. As with a number of our products, we are the sole providers of this glassware, which is also available in amber.

Photograph by Jeffrey Stevensen Photography, courtesy of Churchill Events

Photograph by Brian Phillips Photography

Above and left: We are extremely philanthropic in the community, and one of the organizations dear to our hearts is the Boston Ballet. In its gorgeous studio building in the south end of Boston, high tables, diamond-studded cushion covers created by our in-house interior designer, midnight glassware, and dry ice impart a cool place for patrons to eat lunch amidst a Nutcracker theme. We used our plum halo champagne glasses and stunning serving pieces for an afterparty.

Facing page: A bar mitzvah at Belmont Country Club in Massachusetts featured custom chair backs with velvet ruching, smoke glassware, and luxurious linens for an elegant ambience. As with every event by Carol Silverston of The Original Touch, she brilliantly combined products in the most beautiful and artistic way.

Photograph by Brian Phillips Photography

Photograph by Paul Camello Photography

"New England's incredible,
beautifully executed celebrations
leave everyone feeling honored to
be involved."

—Simone Williamson

Photograph by Paul Camello Photography

Above and left: A private island on Lake Winnipesaukee, New Hampshire, was the perfect setting for a bat mitzvah, albeit a bit challenging. All of the equipment had to be transported in our 24-foot truck on a 45-minute barge excursion, but Amy Piper of Signature Events immaculately executed every detail. Custom furniture with tabletops that we built, stained, and sealed, along with lotus china, veranda black glassware, stylish linens, and Chiavari barstools helped create the modern, youthful atmosphere.

Facing page: A charming venue was transformed into a fashionable lounge area where guests could relax away from the lively party. Like we do at many events, we created and built furniture to fit the space. Fabric boxes, cushions, and our signature tabletops were transformed into comforting vignettes in one area while a unique, artistic mobile of razor blades was surrounded by a circular table and its gorgeous shimmering linens in a separate area.

Photograph by Brian Phillips Photography

Photograph by Brian Phillips Photography

"A close partnership with other professionals is the only way to a truly successful event."

—Simone Williamson

Right: An intimate winter setting aboard a train called for a stylish ambience. Our mahogany astor chair, romance linens, and Milano gold glassware help forge the refined ambience.

Facing page: In keeping with the tones of the magnificent mosaic on display at the Currier Museum in New Hampshire, we collaborated with Amy Piper of Signature Events to create a rich, warm table setting. Amber gazebo glassware and vanessa china perfectly complement the regal red linens.

Photograph by Birch Blaze Photography

views

With so many different options available in creating a beautiful event, it is essential to establish a budget before beginning to consider any of the other details. Otherwise, it's easy to become overwhelmed. After determining at least a range of costs to stay within, the event professionals can better determine what elements will converge to create the best, most appropriate event possible.

PORT LIGHTING SYSTEMS
TODD GERRISH

As a performing musician, Todd Gerrish developed a keen awareness of the impact of good lighting many years ago. The son of an abstract artist and an electrical engineer, he started his career in lighting in 1985 out of his parents' garage, then moved to a school bus that his band once used, and then set up shop in a small warehouse. After honing his skills providing lighting for local bands, he progressed to national recording artists touring through New England, and today his Port Lighting Systems design repertoire includes corporate and special events.

Early on in his career, Todd surrounded himself with a trio of guys—first Paul Fitzgerald, then Bob Harrman and Scott Hunt—who worked with Todd to blaze the trails then and continue to inspire him now, supporting the efforts of the whole company. These days, Paul heads up rentals and repairs, serving as the expert on making things work even better than the manufacturer intended. Bob is the equipment acquisition master, always abreast of the latest and greatest so that when a staff lighting designer asks him how to accomplish even the most outlandish of designs, he quickly responds with a handful of solutions. Scott is the logistics guru, quietly organizing the unbelievable volume of manpower and equipment needed to execute each of the team's events.

Todd and his creative team pride themselves on their high level of service, attention to detail, and innovation—always using cutting-edge equipment like energy-efficient LED lighting or working with existing equipment in ways that achieve maximum impact. They also take pride in consistency, addressing small and large projects with equal importance. Their passion for lighting design is evident even from the earliest phases of collaboration, when they prepare three-dimensional pre-visualizations, and of course at the event itself.

At the Storybook Ball, a fundraiser for Massachusetts General Hospital, we projected jungle-themed images on a white muslin surface, which, coupled with colored pattern projection throughout the space, tied everything together. Lighting design led by Mike Gionfriddo.

Photograph by Aviran Levy

Above: For a Hollywood-themed party in a large tent, we used digital lighting to project collages onto the ceiling. Movie clips played within the collages, which made the ceiling come alive. Lighting design led by Jim Rood.

Facing page: We can accommodate any theme for any party. At a breast cancer fundraiser, we made templates from the pink ribbon symbol and projected them onto the walls to emulate wallpaper. For a Mary Poppins theme, a light haze creates a lofty feeling. For a Boston College fundraiser, we lit trees around the tent that could be seen through the clear ceiling, highlighting the campus.

"Lighting can make or break not only how an event looks but also how guests feel."

—Todd Gerrish

"With even the most basic equipment, creative people flourish. Add a few state-of-the-art elements and the possibilities are endless."
—Todd Gerrish

A fundraiser for the Big Brother Big Sister of Massachusetts Bay organization had an '80s rock band theme, so we used haze and a lot of moving light beams to create that big lighting rig look. For an American Heart Association fundraiser, we utilized hanging lightbulbs and scaffolding to draw out an industrial look. Lighting design led by Mike Gionfriddo.

Photograph by Matt Teuten Photography

Right: At a Las Vegas-themed event, LED panels created an interesting proscenium at the stage displaying abstract video content while theatrical lighting enhanced dinner. Lighting design led by Jim Rood.

Facing page: We projected flowers on the walls at a corporate fundraiser to bring out the essence of spring. Pin spots on the tables added drama to the room and drew attention to the floral centerpieces. For an event at the Boston Public Library, LED uplighting accentuated the building's regal architecture while slowly changing colors.

views

Always explore your options and think them through. Sometimes an idea that sounds crazy and off-the-wall can be turned into something cool and innovative. That's where a lot of our best ideas originate.

TABLE TOPPERS OF NEWTON

EILEEN SALIBA

Specialty linen offers the discerning host a unique design opportunity. It can emphasize one's appreciation for sumptuous elegance or cool minimalism, help express intimacy, be gracious or playful. When designing for exquisitely appointed spaces, linen needs to be meticulously precise. Complement and not compete. Linen's role is to serve as the perfect backdrop for each design element.

At Table Toppers of Newton, fabrics reside in every corner and design inspiration is abundant. Eileen Saliba has owned and operated the company for over 20 years, and in that time she has become a leader in an evolving industry. What was once limited to standard tablecloths, napkins, and chair covers has now become an explosion of patterns, textures, and colors. The ability to enhance and bring an event designer's vision to life is only one part of what Table Toppers expertly offers. Discovering new trends and stocking the hottest styles in its 12,000-square-foot warehouse is how Table Toppers has remained the final word in linen.

Taking cues from the fashion industry and traveling the globe to attend textile shows and exhibitions translates into some seriously chic fabric. Impeccable craftsmanship is a Table Toppers hallmark, and keeping focused solely on linen has allowed its team to become textile experts. It's not uncommon for Eileen and her team to help create generation after generation of celebrations for a single family, accompanying a woman through her bat mitzvah, wedding, baby shower, and daughter's bat mitzvah. Table Toppers just inspires that kind of loyalty.

Placing runners in opposite directions not only helps to showcase details, but also turns them into placemats. Fabric that sits on top of the table gets covered by plates and glassware, while any fabric that hangs down the sides is unencumbered to the eye. Table and floral design by Domenic Cambio Event Design; lighting design by Suzanne B. Lowell Lighting Design; rentals by Tommy Wholesale.

Photograph by Ron Manville

Photograph by Ron Manville

Photograph by Ron Manville

"Fabric makes an enormous contribution to the design of an event. From the beginning, understand the role you want your linens to play."

—Eileen Saliba

Right and facing page: We saw this adorable fabric at a textile show and couldn't resist it! Domenic Cambio of Domenic Cambio Event Design took his inspiration from the fabric and staged a party for the pups at a local animal shelter. Kibble centerpieces and personalized doggy bone placecards made this the perfect playful pooch-inspired design—we even crafted the birthday hats and coats.

Previous pages: Chair covers are a show-stopping way to complete the design, while placecard tables are a terrific outlet for elaborate creativity. With no chairs to block the fabric, a designer's imagination can play with a myriad of concepts.

Photograph by Ron Manville

views

It's very important to understand the process when working with a linen vendor. After you choose the design, color, and fabric, you owe it to yourself to explore the details. Ask how the linens are delivered, if they're pressed, and by whom. What happens if your guest count goes up the day before your event? Take advantage of the unbelievable choices and options for every budget, but don't forget to ask these vital questions.

WINSTON FLOWERS

DAVID WINSTON | TED WINSTON

What began as a pushcart of flowers on Newbury Street first wheeled out by father and son Robert and Maynard Winston in 1944 has evolved into a pioneering boutique located on that same street. Third-generation owners David and Ted Winston are dedicated to long-held Winston ideals of hard work, ingenuity, entrepreneurship, and a family legacy.

Today Winston Flowers encompasses the original neighborhood shop as well as six others, plus a state-of-the-art floral design studio in Boston's South End—the creative heart of the city. The converted industrial building houses a community of top-notch floral specialists. Sourced from special local growers and suppliers worldwide, fresh flowers arrive seven days a week and a constant stream of delivery trucks come and go with myriad Winston creations.

Winston Flowers' legendary special events design is where the firm really shines. The design team has helped expand the already formidable reputation beyond Boston to elite clientele across New England. While fashioning lavish, one-of-a-kind, chic floral displays is the first love of the capable designers, they also visualize and execute entire event aesthetics. These cohesive approaches stimulate all the senses for truly show-stopping presentations. The designers employ the most unique product of the season in these temporary environments while attending to each creative challenge and every minute detail with panache and precision. With inspiration culled from travel, magazines, interior design, architecture, and fashion, the level of quality is some of the freshest around.

For a pre-holiday party at the Institute of Contemporary Art Boston we chose a deep, dark, sexy vibe with reds, blacks, and a touch of reflective silver and platinum. Guests were visually stimulated, whether looking at the impressive video wall, which was designed to conceal theater seating, or enjoying panoramic views of the winter moon rising over the harbor. Sensuous crimson chandeliers hovered over stylized red amaryllis bursting from Italian glass urns and ornamental orbs.

Photograph by Snap!

Above and right: We created a chic, ethereal huppah in the Four Seasons ballroom for a couple who once wished to be wed by the sea. To support the lightness of the design, we masked the heavy architectural features and upholstered walls. We draped the room in white voile, through which refreshing eucalyptus-colored LED projections emanated. Elaborate but simple, the 10-foot-tall structure was constructed from high-gloss faux bois; hundreds of hand-blown glass pieces filled with water were suspended at alternating heights from a mirrored grid overhead. Cattleya orchids for opulence, gloriosa lilies for lyricism, and fuji mums to resemble some aquatic element rounded out the airy effect.

Facing page: For an intimate affair, we developed an art installation within Boston's Institute of Contemporary Art's theater. Three huge picture frames hung from the ceiling with a graphic design of white French tulips and pussy willows that created a weeping willow effect. The shadow of the full "Tree of Life" triptych was projected onto a scrim wall in shadow, creating an impressive arboreal image to complement the series of floral chandeliers. Visually anchored by a natural fiber rug, the 30-foot-long dining table of acrylic and reclaimed wood featured a floating hedge of orchids and hydrangea.

Photograph by Snap!

Right: For DIFFA, we created a rooftop garden setting in an exotic vertical garden. Bromeliads, rhipsalis, coral fern, and privet berries cascaded from a 15-foot botanical structure. Designed in our studio, the acrylic table allowed the diners to view botanical elements submerged in water. To support the water element, we created aquatic gardens in red Domani vessels boasting tall stalks of papyrus illuminated with LEDs.

Facing page: Organic chic qualities set the tone for a winter event in a Vermont barn, compartmentalized into dining and dancing spaces. A series of mirrored pedestals combining Belgian glass with white anemones floating in water blurred the line between reflection and reality; blue light projections highlighted the architecture. We hand-forged wrought iron chandeliers with an eclectic collection of found glass objects with anemones. Glass antlers holding candles ran the length of the reclaimed ipe stained tables, while alternating mirrors and silvan bouquets of paphiopedilum orchids, Sharon fern, moss, and pussy willow chaining appeared throughout the miniature hemlock cone runner.

views

In creating environments for life's celebrations, there is nothing more rewarding than revealing the end results to our clients and sharing that emotional moment when they experience the actualization of their vision.

APOTHECA FLOWERS

ALYSSA VAN GUILDER

For Alyssa Van Guilder, owner and principal designer at Apotheca Flowers, flowers are more than splashes of color on earth's canvas. For her, they offer an intimate look into people's lives, showcasing personalities, stories, and styles through color, texture, and the combination of unique, natural elements.

Known throughout New England for artistically driven designs, Alyssa and her team value the connection they make with each event host during the consultation process and use that connection to convey the personal story or organizational focus for the event. Drawing from seasonal selections—available locally as well as from weekly visits to the Boston Flower Market—and inspired by the innate beauty of the flowers themselves, the floral palette for each week begins to take shape. Back in Apotheca's studio—located in a charming 1860s train depot that boasts much of its original details and acts as a community gathering space—the flower arrangements come to life through a collaborative process that involves the event host nearly every step of the way.

With a bent toward European concepts, Apotheca's designs exude an earthy elegance expressed through natural elements like mosses, rocks, and twigs and through color groupings similar to what would be found in a garden. The sophisticated style is blended with a slight edge, which is a result of Alyssa's preference to approach flower design as another artistic medium. This ensures that each project focuses on the miraculous aspect of each natural element, showcasing its symbolism and beauty.

A romantic ranunculus in a nest of moss was the perfect arrangement for the ring bearer to hold at a vintage garden-style event. We came up with this design since the host didn't want a typical basket or pillow.

Photograph by Melinda Butler

Photograph by Melinda Butler

Photograph by Austin Trenholm

"Every flower needs a voice; don't let the beauty get lost in the arrangement."

—Alyssa Van Guilder

Right: The combination of elements within a design allows us to perfectly match each arrangement with its event. To keep hot colors from being too bold, we introduced a muted counterpart of antique ivory rose; tropical foliage and vintage glass allude to an Old Havana feel.

Facing page top and bottom left: With a pink palette, which is carried throughout the event, rich champagne offers an elegant touch while an earthy berzellia berry counterbalances the soft textures.

Facing page bottom right: Inside a historic church in Massachusetts, we used discreet vessels filled with hydrangea, astilbe, and rainbow fern on every other pew to allow the location's beauty to speak for itself.

Photograph by Sage Studios Photography

views

A beautiful eventscape is about more than just gorgeous flowers. Pay attention to other details like placecards, table numbers, and favors, and find ways to introduce a personal touch to each element. By thinking stylistically about every aspect, you can achieve a distinct, sensational look.

ARTISTIC BLOSSOMS FLORAL DESIGN STUDIO

KELLY DOLLOFF

Though the connection may not be immediately apparent, floral arrangements and blown glass have a lot in common, at least where Kelly Dolloff is concerned. The founder of Artistic Blossoms Floral Design Studio is a trained artist who used to specialize in the delicate and precise art of coaxing glass into fantastic shapes. Finding limited opportunities on the East Coast after college, Kelly turned to flowers, arranging nature with the same fluidity and quickness she once applied to glass. Now, over 20 years later, Artistic Blossoms has expanded to include two Massachusetts studio locations, with a third set to open in New York City.

By eschewing the retail front and concentrating solely on wedding and event floral design, Artistic Blossoms is free to invest time and care in each person that visits. Tapping into an event's theme or selecting just the right shades to complement a color scheme is only the beginning: Kelly delights in using unique requests and dreams as inspiration for a truly memorable design. Not only will Kelly and her team of seasoned designers craft magnificent arrangements of fresh florals, they can also assist with linens, décor, and any other elements required to tie a room together. On the big day all deliveries are done by designers ready to bestow extra-special care on arrangements that may have settled or shifted during transit. A final once-over on everything from centerpieces to boutonnières makes all the difference.

The combination of stained glass and standard windows makes designing in the foyer of the historic Daniel Webster Estate a challenge, but lighting specialist Mike Salvati ensured that the tones we chose were complementary. Since the event was a tea given for an Asian VIP, we drew our inspiration from the guest of honor's cultural heritage. Scarlet silk details, miniature Asian figurines, and black linens provided a dramatic backdrop for the floral centerpieces and Japanese flowering quince, displayed in metal dragon stands.

Photograph by Donald Chapelle

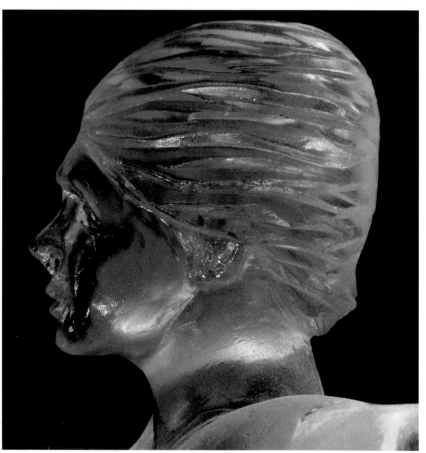

Photograph by Donald Chapelle

Photograph by Donald Chapelle

> "Part of the beauty of an ice sculpture is that it's here today and gone tomorrow."
>
> —Donald Chapelle

Ice can be shaped, molded, and articulated into functional or decorative pieces for any occasion. For Boston's First Night, *Whale Wall* stands in magnificence at dusk and captures the movement of oceanic choreography while the custom margarita bar suggests available drink options, each block representing a different margarita. *Woman's Head* exemplifies the sensuality of human form captured in ice while *Fire and Ice Flame*, a 7-foot-tall centerpiece in a lady's bathroom, absorbs theatrical flicker-flame lighting and refracts it in all directions.

Photograph by Donald Chapelle

views

Ice intensifies the richness of color, the savoriness of fresh herbs and fruit. When the ambience of food translates into the ice experience, guests cannot walk by without smacking their lips and thinking, "Wow, that looks delicious. I want one."

PBD EVENTS

FRANNY ANDAHAZY | MICHAEL NEDEAU

Walking into the offices of PBD Events is like walking into a high-end event. Many of the company's furniture, contemporary accent pieces, and styling props are visible. The areas are organized to facilitate a natural flow, leading prospective hosts through the rooms much like guests are subtly guided through an event. This is not a coincidence.

For many years, Franny Andahazy, Michael Nedeau, and Michelle Gubitosa have been carefully crafting an experience, continually expanding what was originally a prop and event rental business named Party By Design. Now 25 years in business and owned and operated by Franny and Michael, the company is known as PBD Events, a full-service event design and production company specializing in high-end rentals and custom fabrication of event products.

PBD is known for its ability to tackle challenges, or, as Franny would say, being the only people crazy enough to attempt what others might deem impossible. But not only does PBD attempt, it succeeds. The company has built its reputation on being the only one that can find, build, repurpose, or customize just about anything. Working always as a team, the diverse group of artists, writers, builders, thinkers, and visionaries never takes individual credit for its creations. With roughly 700 events a year, that's an astonishing amount of innovation turned into tangible products. Keeping close tabs on the latest industry trends has allowed PBD to evolve and adapt over the years, guaranteeing fresh challenges for many more years to come.

Working in conjunction with Winston Flowers, we took the contemporary interior of the Institute of Contemporary Art and accented the room with our Lucite mirage chairs and custom-built mirrored tables to reflect the incredible nighttime Boston skyline.

"We need to be the people who can make things happen when others cannot."

—Franny Andahazy

Top right: Boston is a city full of history, and it's always a treat to mix contemporary, eclectic furniture and décor like white patent leather ottomans within a downtown loft space that's already full of character.

Bottom right: Within The Park Plaza Castle in downtown Boston, we built a 100-foot skate ramp for an event for Converse. Building something ultra-specialized like that is what we're known for—tackling design challenges is the most exciting part of our job.

Facing page: The concept of teamwork is not restricted to our office; we love collaborating with other vendors and think that the results are often tenfold what one company could have achieved on its own. It's important to let the best do what they do best. Winston Flowers is a company we have worked with frequently and love to collaborate with on designs. These shadowbox tables fabricated by PBD added a unique element to the event. Together with the help of Suzanne B. Lowell Lighting Design's illumination of Winston's florals, the event design created a cohesive feel at the Four Seasons.

views

Going green in our industry is not very difficult if one is conscious about it. Reusing and repurposing items over and over is the very essence of customization. Taking something like the wooden sign from one event and making into a lounge table for another not only reduces cost but gives materials another, longer life.

Photograph by Rafanelli Events

Photograph by Tables of Content Catering

Photograph by Person + Killian Photography

Photograph by Frank Giuliani

"You can rent items from many sources, but the right people are the key to a successful event."

—Bob Traina

Right: In downtown Boston, a tent with clear roof panels and solid walls gave guests a fantastic view of the John Hancock Tower and shielded the event activities from the eyes of passersby. We designed the flooring around the existing trees to accommodate the one-of-a-kind location.

Facing page top left and bottom right: A variety of tents are available to suit nearly any kind of event, whether it's a small backyard barbecue with a canopy tent for 10, a large company event with multiple peaked tension tents for nearly 1,000, or a high-end gala located in a public setting.

Facing page top right and bottom left: From traditional elements to the more contemporary and everything in between, the array of equipment and décor available for special events is almost unimaginable.

views

Just like the top three rules of real estate are location, location, location, the top three rules of hosting an event are planning, planning, planning. When it comes to your big day, there is only one surefire way to make sure it all goes off without a hitch: have a plan, and then have a backup plan, and then have a backup plan for the backup plan.

Photograph by Florence McCall

Photograph by Sayles Livingston

Photograph by Alexandria Mauck

"It's not solely about awe-inspiring designs; it's about injecting personality into them."

—Sayles Livingston

Right and facing page bottom: I love to use flowers in unusual ways, especially as a table covering for the sweetheart table or cake table, a flower girl's skirt, a lush shawl, a dress train, or a bolero jacket. Unique pairings of floral elements, such as combining lush flowers with succulents, ferns, and berries, also provides a fresh twist on the traditional florals.

Facing page top: To elicit an organic, romantic atmosphere I designed a shimmering woodland oasis with topiaries made of birch trees and a few flowers for a pop of color, hemstitch natural linen overlays, and twinkle lights.

Photograph by Sayles Livingston

views

To begin thinking about flowers and event décor, visit the local hardware store and choose a few paint swatches that really speak to you. Browse through magazines—but don't only look through wedding or event publications. Seek out interior design, architecture, and fashion magazines to see a broader range of designs. Then you and your florist can use the styles and colors you're attracted to as a foundation for selecting the décor.

"Flowers are the perfect tools for creating art; their perfection and beauty are unrivaled."

—Orly Khon

Right: We interspersed low arrangements of roses and lisianthus with fabulous blooming branches for a soft, romantic feel, all enhanced by red lighting.

Facing page left: With only 50 guests, Tangorra Wedding Planning envisioned something dramatic and modern. We paired the clean lines of blooming branches with multiple arrangements of a singular flower—roses, calla lilies, and hydrangea—and unified the entire design with a custom silver table runner.

Facing page right: Seemingly opposing styles can work together in unique ways. At a summer fête, we embraced bright colors with a subtle tropical feel and textually fun elements to evoke a contemporary yet non-minimalist look. For an event orchestrated by Unique Weddings by Alexis, long-stemmed calla lilies uniquely arranged in nearly invisible vases impart a modern yet classic feel.

Photograph by Zev Fisher Photography

views

❖ Every floral creation is a work of art that requires a careful balance between the color, shape, and intended impact.

❖ Don't be afraid of the budget. Often, it's even more pleasing to the eye to do more with less by making a statement through a singular color or a simple dramatic effect.

"No idea is too old or too new…
it's good to always bring a fresh
approach to every event."
—Neal Balkowitsch

Presenting food in an unusual or uncommon way turns the tasty morsels into not only the main attraction but also a part of the décor. Displaying pickled vegetables in glass canisters or standing lobster salad ficelle crisp sandwiches upright in shot glasses is playful and anything but standard.

"Two things to remember about an event: make it great and make it you."

—Dan Mathieu

Right and facing page: Sushi-grade salmon garnished with crudo-shaved radish, kumquat, vanilla salt, and micro celery dots a plate with color, while lobster and artichoke on herbed falafel with carrot tuile takes the presentation skyward. While they love to get inventive in the kitchen, our chefs can be immaculate with details, such as when they are plating butter-poached lobster, seared scallops, pommes purée, and beet gastrique.

Previous pages: Nestled inside the nooks and crannies of a bookcase was an array of sweet little surprises: panna cotta with guava caramel, hazelnut gâteau, Russian tea cakes, chocolate tortes, ganache French macaroons, marcona almond mousse cake, and ice cream sundaes with salted peanut brittle.

views

We like to challenge people to be grand. These events celebrate some of the most meaningful moments in your life, and you want to be able to look back and still be wowed by how it all turned out.

TABLES OF CONTENT CATERING

STEPHEN BARCK | LINDA DE FRANCO BARCK

Fulfilling his dream of delivering awe-inspiring cuisine and service that leaves guests in applause, Stephen Barck opened Tables of Content Catering in 1992. Linda De Franco joined the team in 1995 to handle sales management; the two discovered a shared passion for excellence and soon married. Today Tables of Content thrives under Stephen and Linda's joint ownership thanks to a never-ending pursuit of perfection, a commitment to exceeding expectations, an unparalleled supply of inspired cuisine, and a dedication to operating with integrity and keeping promises.

Passion. Energy. Flair. That's what the catering and event planning company brings to the table for every event, large or small, lavish or modest. Personal attention and green practices are the two core ingredients. Stephen and Linda are intimately involved in the day-to-day running of the business, with Stephen the culinary artist composing exquisite menus and personally catering on-location and Linda the event planner and consultant bringing visions to life. The only certified green caterer in Massachusetts, Tables of Content—all too aware that the food industry is a big energy consumer—utilizes as many innovative steps and processes as possible to keep it lean and green. A successful 150-plant herb garden has brought fresh, organic nature and a smaller carbon footprint to the company, and a zero-waste event initiative promises future commendation.

The result is unmatched flavor and quality delivered by a dynamic fleet of well-trained employees passionate about flawless service—the team regularly takes the level of quality from above-average to truly world-class. After all, Stephen and Linda's compassion goes beyond clientele alone and extends to the diligent staff as well. The couple truly feels fulfilled by each host and guest's thrilled reaction to the company's faithful interpretation of the vision, which is guaranteed to go beyond even wildest dreams.

I've always taken pride in my ability to bring pleasure to people through good food. Silver skewers of tenderloin with a béarnaise sauce accompanied by fresh herbs made a delectable passed hors d'oeuvre at a tasting.

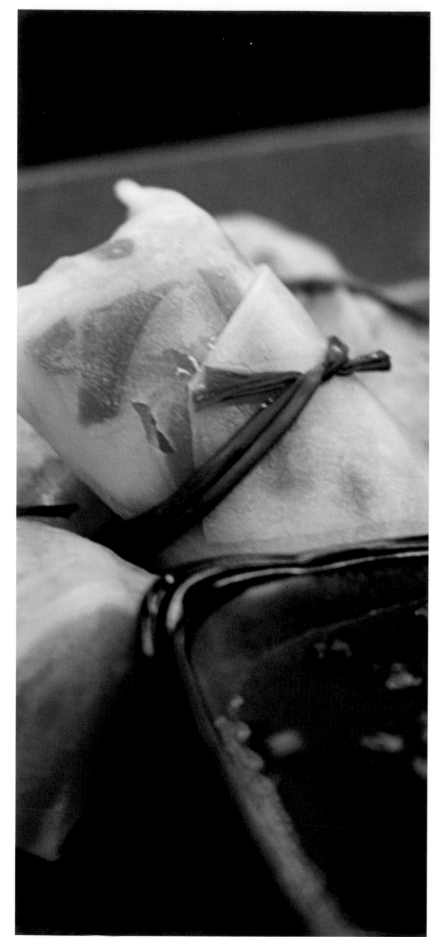

"Consistency is our claim to fame. As a chef-owned company, our food will still taste just as good a year in the future as it did on the day of the tasting."

—Stephen Barck

Fresh Thai spring rolls with nuoc cham dipping sauce, grilled teres major with charred vidalia onion, beef jus, and satin mashed potatoes, and artisan vegetable terrine wrapped in leeks made from organic spring vegetables are just a few examples of what our kitchen regularly whips up on demand.

"From the menu to the place settings to the music, everything needs to gel. By listening and anticipating needs, visions transform into catered spectacles."

—Linda De Franco Barck

Above: Food must please the eye as well as the palate. Whimsical food entertains our hosts and guests on all levels. Artfully carved vegetables playfully garnish trays and help set a romantic tone.

Facing page: Passed hors d'oeuvres can take many forms, from whiskey-barbecued duck with summer peach relish in Asian soup spoons to an herbed grilled cheese and tomato soup shooter to Turkish apricots stuffed with gorgonzola and figs.

Photograph courtesy of Tables of Content

Photograph courtesy of Tables of Content

Right: Tilapia stuffed with lemon saffron risotto in a tomato bouillon and topped with frizzled leeks makes a show-stopping entrée.

Facing page: Squash pots accompanied by nuts and cranberries will soon be filled with roasted butternut squash soup, while an elaborate sushi display entertains the eyes as well as the taste buds.

views

❖ A good sign of a worthwhile caterer is fresh food chosen with an eye to the season.

❖ Pooling resources and collaborative communication with colleagues is absolutely key.

❖ Highly trained chefs with years of experience, a love of food, and a genuine desire to send events soaring will produce aû courant, imaginative, creative fare.

The Catered Affair

HOLLY SAFFORD | ANDREW MARCONI | ALEX MARCONI

Things can never be too perfect. At least that's the philosophy of the team at The Catered Affair, led by Holly Safford and her sons Andrew and Alex Marconi. With more than three decades of catering and design expertise, The Catered Affair has become synonymous with flawless events. From the highest quality ingredients and innovative design to the way waitstaff treats guests, the team incorporates an unprecedented attention to detail and a near-obsession with perfection.

Holly and her energetic staff focus on creating fresh, innovative dishes for their always-custom menus and on designing events that reflect the host's personalities and goals. No matter what the celebration involves, hosts and guests experience an unparalleled commitment to excellence, from the initial planning session until the last plate is washed and put away, making the process not just about a meal but about an exceptional experience.

The Catered Affair hasn't always been what it is today, although perfection has consistently been at its core. It all started from Holly's need to support her young sons after a divorce and her friends' career suggestions based on her love of—and talent in—entertaining. Armed with little other than passion, bravery, and a knack for cooking, Holly has grown the company from its beginnings in her kitchen to a renowned catering and design business with 50 full-time staff, including an amazing executive chef—Matthew Donegan—and an insightful event and floral designer—Ed Quinones.

The ambience of an event is irrevocably intertwined with the cuisine. While we don't try to compete with event designers, sometimes hosts just want a little extra help along with the catering. In a roomy tent, we created a romantic, airy feel with globe lanterns and white linens.

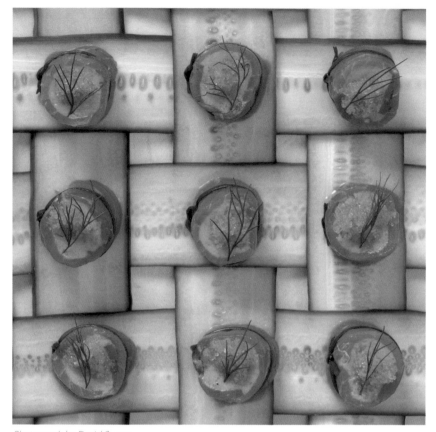

"Inspired cuisine is all about approaching each event with a fresh eye."

—Andrew Marconi

Photograph by David Seaver

Photograph by The Catered Affair

Above left: The quality plays an especially important role in hors d'oeuvres because such a small bite needs to have a big punch, as seen with the Provençal crusted tuna on white bean crostini with micro arugula and parmesan.

Above right: To ensure the quality is up to our high standards, we use organic local ingredients whenever possible. For a delightful summer celebration, we paired a lovely poached native lobster with an apple reduction, a crisp candied apple, a petite herb salad, and chili oil.

Facing page left: Presented atop a cucumber lattice for a stunning display, smoked salmon roulade is topped with salmon mousse, tobiko caviar, and a dill sprig.

Facing page right: A pepper-crusted ahi tuna burger delicately holds a tomato, micro arugula, and garlic aioli on a mini-bun.

"Joy in the planning stages almost always translates to a joyous event."
—Holly Safford

Right: The birthday honoree's passion for shopping prompted a hot pink, fashion-themed party. A larger-than-life ice sculpture of a hot pink high heel pump filled with caviar greeted guests for the cocktail hour. At the November dinner, while "Project Runway's" Tim Gunn hosted a fashion show, guests enjoyed delicious seasonal dishes: autumnal salad, a filet of beef, basil-whipped potatoes, and a warm chocolate bomb with "happy birthday" inscribed in chocolate on each plate. Flowers by Winston Flowers; decor in collaboration with PBD Events.

Facing page: The presentation, whether of the cuisine or of the event itself with the ambience, is foundational to how a guest will feel at the event. For example, vibrant colors in the fare and in the décor add an upbeat energy to a space.

Photograph by Winslow Martin

views

Having the appropriate number of staff to attend to the guests and to execute the event according to the host's goals is essential. The food's quality is of course just as important, but there are ways to create delicious meals on a smaller budget. Unfortunately there's just no way to cut back on service with the same results.

Russell Morin Fine Catering

Russell Morin

Topiary camels flanking the entrance to a Moroccan-inspired award show and artistically painted servers at an octogenarian's glitz and glam birthday party are not generally the first things that come to mind when discussing a caterer. But those are precisely the types of unexpected elements that tie the menu of scrumptious fare to the event's theme. The result? A wholly delectable and unforgettable experience. Russell Morin Fine Catering's expert event coordinators are happy to assist with every detail: linens, flowers, musicians, décor and, of course, developing the menu.

While known for signatures like New England clam chowder and other coastal cuisine, the fourth-generation, 1911-established company Russell Morin Fine Catering has vast expertise and cuisine that spans every continent, style, and school. Believing that superb food can be made even better by adding just the right finishing touch, like a dollop of crème fraîche, a sprig of rosemary, or perhaps a curl of ginger, the chefs consider absolutely every detail when planning menus and preparing meals. They have a diverse repertoire of appetizers, entrées, and desserts, each one enhancing the senses as well as teasing the palate for what is to come.

Each event is unique, but all possess a certain signature style—a smooth combination of creative ideas, extraordinary food, gracious service, and impeccable attention to detail. Whether serving up caviar and champagne or pizza and lemonade, the catering team does so with flair.

A stunning clear tent, rustic tables, birch and oak trellises, hanging antique glass, and iron votives greeted guests at a midsummer's wedding reception on the grounds of a beautiful Massachusetts estate. We invoked the ambience of an alfresco Tuscan-style wedding by complementing the earthy yet elegant décor with a menu that celebrated the essence of Italian culinary tradition.

Photograph by Sarah Bastille Photography

"The locavore theme—farm to table, from just down the road—has grown from a mere trend to a blossoming movement that continues to gain momentum."

—Russell Morin

Locally grown, colorful, and fragrant floral centerpieces convey the desire to feature sustainable agriculture and the community's culinary artisans. For a mid-spring wedding, a tomato tartare and micro-basil timbale top slices of green zebra and pink brandywine tomatoes. Our contemporary Caesar salad features a bundle of organic romaine lettuce with a chive tie and a creamy parmesan dressing and parmesan crisp.

Photograph by Kristin Spencer Photography

views

Ask the top vendors in the area who they'd recommend. They work with each other and know who does the right job, and they'll give honest feedback. You have to be comfortable working with the vendors—responsiveness is critical.

A THYME TO COOK

LINDA SAMPLE

Nestled in the southeastern Connecticut countryside, surrounded by farm-fresh ingredients, award-winning chefs are hard at work and play, inventing culinary creations that express their limitless creativity and sense of adventure. Linda Sample, resident gourmand and A Thyme to Cook's visionary founder, believes that great food should appeal to your taste buds as well as your eyes and imagination. Her catering firm's 25-year-long list of happy hosts and delighted guests proves that her innovative culinary philosophy is a good one.

A Thyme to Cook's first love is creating fabulous fresh food with local ingredients. From start to finish, the culinary team develops customized menus, builds full-service field kitchens, designs the décor and environment, and provides impeccable service—all to create a total guest experience.

Inspired by the opportunity to enhance people's gatherings and celebrations with fine cuisine and perfectly paired wine and specialty drinks, Linda and her team are proud to say that they've never duplicated an event—and never will. Catering events from Boston to New York, they boast hors d'oeuvres, entrées, and desserts that are as refreshing and sassy as their studio's architecture: a rustic wood structure with a bright purple door, surrounded by a field of aromatic fresh herbs.

For an elegant, sophisticated entrée, seared sea bass sits atop a mango mojo and is topped with a microgreen salad of red cabbage and fennel.

Photograph by Christine Keene

Photograph by Robert Norman

Photograph by Robert Norman

Photograph by Robert Norman

"Creativity is the most important ingredient."

—Linda Sample

For a fundraising gala at the Branford House Mansion on the University of Connecticut campus, we provided a variety of hors d'oeuvres. Such dishes as golden raspberry cream caramel with curled tangles and wisps of pulled sugar appeal to the sweet tooth. Crisped basil leaves garnish twin soup with curried coconut pearls. Practicing molecular gastronomy is the best way to invent exciting new dining experiences .

views

The key to a smooth operation is a great team of people who are highly trained, flexible, and have the ability to think on their feet. New England is riddled with sudden weather changes. We pride ourselves on being able to make last minute adjustments to menus and logistics in order to assure guests' comfort.

CAKES TO REMEMBER

ELLEN BARTLETT

Chocolate and vanilla have long ranked at the top of the favorite flavors list, but when they are up against magical concoctions like strawberry orange blossom, lemon satin, and deep chocolate framboise, the straightforward classics are quickly overtaken. As a baker, an artist, and the proprietor of Cakes to Remember, Ellen Bartlett is celebrated for her innovative flavor combinations and creative approach, which ensure unique desserts that look as fabulous as they taste—and vice versa.

The world would simply be a better place if every business meeting commenced with casual conversation and concluded with a few slices of gourmet cake, and that's precisely how Ellen works. She loves visiting with people about their flavor ideas and aesthetic preferences and discussing the cake's role as the visual centerpiece of social affairs—it really does tie everything together. Once the look and taste have been defined, Ellen takes care of all the details related to sizing, preparation, and delivery, coordinating brilliantly with whomever the event host appoints.

Ellen's passion for baking has been steadily growing since she was a little girl. She made her first wedding cake for her sister while attending Brown University; shortly after graduating, she formally ventured into the culinary arts. In 1988, after 10 years of cooking professionally and making cakes for friends, she decided to narrow her focus to something fun that gave her creative freedom and Cakes to Remember was born.

Today well-known for her incredibly detailed handwork, Ellen is adept at a variety of artistic mediums, from buttercream to rolled fondant and marzipan, and she continues to redefine the possibilities of cake design.

Working with an event planner, we designed a groom's cake for a bride who had found her prince. The groom was a chef, so the royal frog came equipped with the tools of his trade.

"Done elegantly and with good taste, a combination of color, balance, and form lifts a cake into the realm of sculpture."

—Ellen Bartlett

The right cake will personalize the occasion, such as a small but special roulette wheel and cards—a birthday cake for someone who loves casinos. A fun tropical forest cake was a hit for a little girl's jungle-themed birthday party while a royal egg for a Russophile authenticated the art gallery birthday party. For the 25th anniversary of the Boston Lyric Opera, an assortment of performance hats emerged from a huge Dr. Seuss hat box, and for a sweet sixteen, seven tiers encased in flames and replete with the seven deadly sins nodded to Dante's *Inferno*, truly one hell of a cake.

Photograph by Ellen Bartlett

views

Cake inspiration can come from so many different sources—experiences, travels, interests, favorite themes, places, a love of ribbons and bows, anything really. The secret to coming up with the perfect look for a cake is fearlessly exploring what makes you or your event special and then using flavor and artistry to showcase that uniqueness.

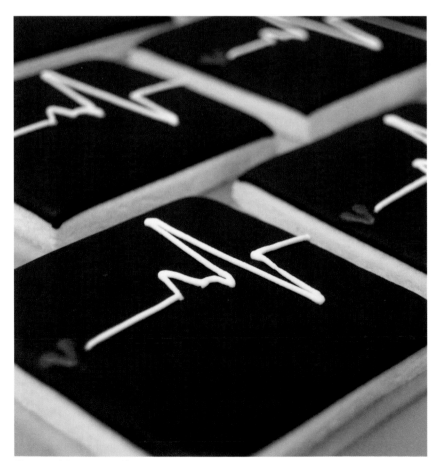

"Decorated cookies are so versatile. Whether served at an event or given as party favors, the possibilities are endless!"

—Jennifer Burkhart

Presented on the sweet table or wrapped in cellophane with ribbon as take-home treats, decorated cookies always captivate guests. I piped lily of the valley on three-inch rounds for a proper bridal tea party. My paisley-shaped design artfully tops a scoop of gelato. By recreating brand logos or elegant monograms, cookies become placecard holders to personalize an event. Even an ocean theme is inspiration; I piped dots of royal icing in hues of blue, then hand-painted some with edible silver luster dust. Tiny clear acrylic easels support each cookie masterpiece.

Photograph by Justin Burkhart

views

Bring your ideas to the table, but allow your professional decorating expert to offer new ways to add sparkle to your event. Cookies provide a great opportunity to pull in a custom logo or expand your party theme. Allow about six weeks' lead time to have your cookies designed and to develop packaging. It's all about customizing your order and discovering the perfect presentation.

On 20

NOEL JONES

An On 20 meal is a legend with a place on every gourmand's bucket list, and for good reason. The ingredients are local, organic, and fresh; the chefs armed with expertise and spontaneity, aware that the same dish is never prepared twice even from one recipe. Special event guests and hosts who attend affairs at the restaurant or recruit the chefs to prepare food in their own homes come away breathless and awed.

Executive chef Noel Jones helms a passionate team intent on perfection and excellence. Dishes are inspired by seasonally available ingredients and chefs often build an entire plate around one well-formed specimen, letting the beauty of the raw food inspire the cooking method. The chefs make up a cohesive team who regularly act as sounding boards for ideas, leading to a collaborative decision. No classic recipe is off-limits; it can always be reinvented and transformed into the creative star of a tasting menu. High-quality food products and equipment are at the core of the craft. The result is mouthwateringly delectable cuisine that's the talk of Hartford.

No matter whether guests are being served On 20 fare in the home restaurant or in their own homes, every detail is accounted for. From the direction the plate is facing when set before the diner by the server to supposedly simple tasks like chopping vegetables, every member of the team brings a single-minded dedication. Chef Noel emphasizes to his staff that the present moment is more important than the past or the future: the dishes must be at their best every day. Constantly changing and evolving in response to feedback and information, the team is flexible and versatile. While the view from the restaurant's vantage point of the 20th floor is gorgeous, the real show is what's on the plates—and guests love to be surprised by the innovation and freshness they discover.

Artichoke ragout is a fresh, exciting dish symbolizing early spring, with vegetables in harmony. Baby carrots, haricots verts, radishes, herbs, a flower garnish, and some crispy dehydrated French ham—accented by dots of basil coulis—combine into one elegantly formed plate.

Photograph by Diana DeLucia

Photograph by Diana DeLucia

"Nourishment is our foremost duty. The focus should be on feeding guests, not the chef's ego."

—Noel Jones

Right: Tasting menus take our guests on a journey; diners traverse a veritable sea of plates whipped up from the chef's expertise and the season's offerings.

Facing page: Everything we do is infused with ingenious creativity. From a *baccalà* salt cod and potato chip confection topped with squid ink and fleur de sel to Spanish octopus atop sous-vide potato and saffron rouille to sea urchin royale crowning a beach of edible sand to a caramel custard pastry made to look like a nest, our creations are appealing in both appearance and taste.

views

❖ Give guests a sense of surprise and excitement by withholding explicit descriptions of the dish from the menus.

❖ In the kitchen, if the proposed dish doesn't work when it goes on the plate, change it.

❖ Push the envelope when it comes to customer service and meal presentation.

WILD ORCHID BAKING COMPANY

ERIN GARDNER

Just as its legendary namesake bloom sprang from a couple's love, Wild Orchid Baking Company stems from pastry chef Erin Gardner's passion for creating custom cakes and pastries that are as visually interesting as they are delicious. Known for its special event cakes, the bakery's shelves are lined daily with fresh cupcakes and other delights, all baked from scratch using the finest ingredients, and always pure butter. With its grand opening in 2009, Wild Orchid Baking Company has already earned a devoted following and numerous industry accolades.

Erin states that the key to the bakery's success is the level of customization she and her team are able to bring to each cake project they undertake. She gets to know each client, divining every important event detail, and then lets the creative process unfold. Whether a sculptural, three-tiered wedding cake adorned with Wild Orchid's signature sugar flowers or bringing the Force to the table with a whimsical Yoda cake, Erin and her team imbue each delectable creation with the patron's personality.

Viewing her artistically intricate pastries, it's easy to see that this truly is Erin's calling. She has a unique ability to envision a design that beautifully complements the event costume and décor, integrating each cake into the scene while simultaneously making a powerful statement that's both seen and tasted. For Erin, custom baking is creativity with a purpose; it combines design, flavor, and service to delicious effect.

Creating a sophisticated, modern cake can be challenging—frosting isn't the ideal medium for clean, precise lines. We've perfected the art of sculpting sugar into highly detailed floral accents that match the arrangements and can even defy gravity.

Photograph by Michael Woytek

Photograph by Jay Drinker, Drinker Images

Photograph by Jay Drinker, Drinker Images

Photograph by Michael Woytek

Photograph by Michael Woytek

"The best cake designs happen when you step back and let the creative process work."

—Erin Gardner

Right: Inspiration can take many forms, and with it comes a range of challenges. A cake inspired by a Marimekko fabric required that each floral detail be accurately handcrafted then appliquéd to the cake surface.

Facing page: Working in New England allows us a variety of creative opportunities. From clambakes and nautical-themed events to children's birthday parties, unique themes inspire some of the most exciting designs. From fondant and sugar paste, we can sculpt everything from the most realistic orchid or sand dollar to the most whimsical crustacean—and the best part is it's all edible!

Photograph by Jay Drinker, Drinker Images

views

When choosing a cake designer, get referrals, request samples, and ask lots of questions—a good designer should be able to answer them all. And the more information you provide your cake designer, the better. The color of your shoes and your dad's boutonnière may seem like minor details to you, but they can have a profound effect on the look of your cake.

À DEUX: BESPOKE BRIDAL PAPER

KELLI R. PARKER

The emotional and spiritual union of two people warrants an appropriate level of pageantry, not only during and after the ceremony but from the very first planning stages. When a couple announces their wedding, the save-the-dates and invitations create momentum for everything that follows. Kelli Parker recognized the importance of such after being disappointed by what was available for her own 2005 wedding. Boring paper, cliché graphics, minimal effort—it all looked the same to her, and it wasn't "special." In desperation, she designed her own stationery and got unexpected rave reviews. Friends, family, and referred strangers starting calling with similar complaints about mainstream invitation offerings, and Kelli decided to create something new. She utilized her professional background in fine art and graphic design as well as her education—degrees in journalism, art, and business from the University of Georgia—and launched a full-time career, founding à deux: bespoke bridal paper.

Bespoke is a primarily European term that pertains to clothing that is tailored to an individual, and Kelli looks at her service to an event as providing a personalized wardrobe of paper. Instead of invitations that are traditionally ordered from a catalog, à deux provides an entirely made-to-measure stationery suite customized through client preferences to be distinct.

A master of the creative process, Kelli listens to what people say and don't say about their unique vision for the much-anticipated celebration. Gently guiding people to designs and ideas that reflect their personalities in a fresh, classy way is what Kelli does best. Each wardrobe is handmade and one-of-a-kind.

Exuding understated elegance, a luscious, extra-wide ivory silk ribbon wraps the chocolate-colored box. Within the custom fur-lined box, I mounted the invitation on silk and secured it with a crystal buckle. The glorious presentation gives the invitees pause and serves as a luxurious keepsake.

Photograph by McBoat Photography

"I want my couples to have something they would have created for themselves, something that makes their guests feel special and excited."
—Kelli R. Parker

Each stationery ensemble is personal to the people that I'm creating it for. That kind of detail is important—to turn a passing thought into something custom and unique. The invitation is the guests' first glimpse of the event to come and a reflection of the couple I've created it for. Some will come to me for all of their wedding paper—I'm happy to coordinate a bespoke stationery wardrobe for an entire event, from save-the-dates to thank you cards.

views

❖ Let etiquette be a guideline, not an unbreakable creative barrier.

❖ A wedding invitation is something your guests are going to keep for a long time. Consider that when thinking about paper, quality, style, and typefaces, and ask yourself what will stand the test of time.

❖ Budgetary restrictions are a real part of every project. I'm always looking for ways to maintain top quality and service while working within my clients' financial boundaries.

EFD Creative — Event Planning & Design
EDNA DRATCH-PARKER

We all know the power of branding in business—but this concept of creating a unique identity, a theme that unifies all elements and underscores a sense of self, turns an ordinary gathering into an unforgettable experience. The gifted principal of EFD Creative has honed this skill, earning the company a distinguishing trademark: The Wedding Brander™.

Indeed, EFD Creative designs and plans weddings and any other event you can imagine. But Edna Dratch-Parker's diverse background allows her to capture and bring visions to life in every aspect of the event. From graphic to fashion design—Edna designed and promoted her own line of swimwear—to advertising, Edna's many talents harmoniously converge to create events that are as extraordinary as each host.

Perhaps more important than her design abilities is Edna's passion for people. Her ability and desire to connect with people allows her to delve into their dreams and realize them visually. She'll become, in essence, your personal designer, distilling your ideas into a simple, consistent theme that expresses the ideal you wish to project.

Though EFD Creative does it all, from securing a venue to coordinating lighting, décor, and floral design, it's the details that really set Edna and her team apart. Invitations, placecards, programs—every element underscores the event's theme and reflects what's really important: the guest of honor.

Good event designers draw inspiration from their surroundings. Living in New England, I enjoy using elements of its history and landscape. Traditional, refined designs with touches of the coast give guests a distinct sense of place.

DR. AND MRS. MORRIS DRATCH
REQUEST THE HONOR OF YOUR PRESENCE
AT THE MARRIAGE OF THEIR DAUGHTER

Edna Françoise

TO

James William

SON OF

MR. AND MRS. JAMES W. PARKER JR.

TURDAY, THE TWENTY-THIRD OF AUGUST

TWO THOUSAND AND EIGHT

AT SIX O'CLOCK IN THE EVENING

NEW SEABURY COUNTRY CLUB

MASHPEE, MASSACHUSETTS

TION IMMEDIATELY FOLLOWING

David Roseman & Leslie Sargent

Mr. and Mr.. James Hallet.

Photograph by Marina Sun, LifeFusion Studio

September 26, 1959

Please join us in celebrating
the 50th wedding anniversary of
Jim & Pat Parker, Jr.

On Saturday, August eighth,
two thousand and nine

Dinner & Dancing

Knights of Columbus Hall
Seventeen Willow Street
Westborough, Massachusetts
Six-thirty in the evening

ed by the Parker children & grandchildren
Please reply by July twentieth
Jim Parker 111 - jwpthirda charter.net
508 278-7401

hotograph you may have of yourself with Jim & Pat
ll be added to a special photo album.
+ dressed in your favorite lifties outfit

Photograph by Marina Sun, LifeFusion Studio

L K

The pleasure of your company is requested
at the marriage of

Luciana and Keith

Sunday the Twentieth of September
Two Thousand and nine
at five thirty in the afternoon

Martha Mary Chapel
Sudbury, Massachusetts

Tion To follow at the Wayside Inn Ballroom

L K

Photograph by Marina Sun, LifeFusion Studio

J B

Mr. & Mrs. Dennis F. Daly and
Captain & Mrs. Lorendo Andrew Cumbie
request the honour of your presence
at the marriage of

Jennifer Anne Daly
to
Benjamin Rushton Cumbie

Saturday, September nineteenth
two thousand and nine
four-o'clock in the afternoon
The Skinner Barn
Waitsfield, Vermont

J B

Blueberry Lake

Photograph by Marina Sun, LifeFusion Studio

"Art speaks to people's emotions. Adding unique artistic touches infuses the design with your personality and engages your guests."

—Edna Dratch-Parker

The invitations set the scene well before the venue doors open. The theme must be clearly articulated the moment guests open the envelope. From the colors to the fonts to the graphics, the elements should work together to draw guests into the world you're creating, whether it's a bygone era, an elegant garden, or a romantic pastoral setting. As a typographer, I understand that the characters are as important as the words they form. Reiterating the typeface in placecards and adding complementary décor to table settings completes the ideal effect. For pieces that need a handmade quality, collaborating with calligrapher Megan Chapin brings them to life.

Photograph by Marina Sun, LifeFusion Studio

views

It's really important to connect with your designer's personality and sense of style. The first meeting is a two-way interview since creative professionals recognize that a strong relationship is the foundation for a successful event. Remember, you're inviting this person into your life for a significant length of time, so the whole process needs to be productive as well as fun.

IMPRESS ME DESIGNS

CELESTE SIMPSON

If you were to ask graphic designer Celeste Simpson's clientele, the name of her business would not be Impress Me Designs—it would be "I'm impressed!" She received those words of feedback so often in the early days before she incorporated her activities into a full-fledged business that when the time came to decide an official name, she resorted to the phrase she'd heard the most. Today it beautifully sums up Celeste's eye-catching designs and superb ability to please.

While the firm was formed in 2005, Celeste's artistic leanings stretch much further back—to childhood, when she frequently drew and studied art, eventually acquiring a degree in graphic design and art. After years of experience in business sectors, Celeste began teaching classes on how to create cards. More and more, her impressed students asked her to simply design the finished product for them. To this day her goal is to leave a lasting impression that allows the design, not the designer, to stand the strongest.

Wedding and party invitations, announcements, thank you notes, greeting cards and stationery, even gifts and favors—all of these are part of the repertoire. Celeste allows her conversations with her patrons to dictate where her inspiration will lead her, and that's often to fun, elaborate embellishments like jewels, crystals, and textures. Detail-oriented and particular, Celeste settles for nothing less than materials that faithfully execute her precise vision, always true to the host's taste and personality. For her, the most gratifying words of praise are to hear, "I love them all; I can't decide" when she presents prospective design options.

To wow a Miami bride who wanted bright, bold colors, silk calla lilies brushed with diamond dust—a flower represented in the wedding bouquet—along with a crimson bow and crystal jeweled buckle set in gold greeted invitees upon opening the saffron boxed invitation.

"Great invitations inspire anticipation and spur you to personally call the host with compliments."

—Celeste Simpson

Right: Whether I'm creating an invitation to a holiday party or to a traditional Greek wedding, I find inspiration all around me. Each year I come up with a new color palette and design for a regular patron's annual holiday party invite, and an elegant boxed wedding invitation set featured crystal accents and die-cut corners for a motif that was continuous throughout the programs, menus, and seating cards.

Facing page: From the first announcements right into the reception, I prepare a full suite of event materials that's unified and consistent. A masculine printed collection boasted silk invitation boxes in a deep aqua hue and quilled, feather-patterned paper; the occasion of a nonprofit donor event meant an attention-getting design was an absolute must; a lake wedding for an outdoorsy couple saw their dog transformed into a graphic element that branded the entire celebration.

views

Good designers have your best interests at heart and aren't afraid to help you discover the best color combinations and font choices so that your printed piece can shine and impress those who receive it. Intent listeners who strive for your positive feedback won't fail to show you something that thrills you.

An invitation sets the party in motion. It leaves guests with a sense of excitement and anticipation. Whether exemplifying chic elegance or unconventional flair, the invitation should convey the spirit of the celebration as well as the hosts' personal style. Fine detailing, custom styling, and novel dimension can leave a lasting impression.

Photograph by Patrick McNamara Photography

views

Invitations should reflect your personal style rather than the trend of the moment. Don't be afraid to break convention and consider using imaginative materials. Guests will be eager to know what awaits inside. Never underestimate the importance of the invitation because receiving it will be a defining moment for everyone on the guest list.

PERSON + KILLIAN PHOTOGRAPHY

JILL PERSON | LAURÉN KILLIAN

Hitting the shutter-release button is just one element of the creative process for Jill Person and Laurén Killian. They are engaged in their work from the moment they meet potential photographic subjects, through the entire photo session or event, and even at the photo finishing stage. It's not that they couldn't use a bit of downtime, they just love doing it all.

Laurén and Jill founded their namesake photography company in 2004, and after working from home for the first year, moved to downtown Boston. Person + Killian Photography, while also shooting corporate events, focuses primarily on weddings and various other social events. Though the firm works mostly in Boston, much of the work comes from New York clientele that go to Newport, Rhode Island, to get married, causing the firm to expand into a second studio in Newport.

Laurén and Jill do everything hands-on. They pride themselves on their colors, understanding the importance of having great saturation to keep the pictures vibrant and capture the emotion of the day. Their style reflects the combination of photojournalism, artistry, and emotion coupled with an innate sense of spontaneity.

For a bat mitzvah under the planning and design of Rafanelli Events, the family imported the feel of their favorite southern France nightclub into a modern ballroom—authentic from floor to ceiling—and we captured the wow factor of entering the room through wonderful lighting and proper exposure.

Photograph by Person + Killian Photography

Photograph by Person + Killian Photography

Shooting in bright sunlight with no shade, we have to work with the light and properly expose the images to capture emotions, details, colors, and concepts.

"The trick to shooting events is taking in the whole scene without missing any of the special details."
—Laurén Killian

"An innovative camera angle and elegant burst of color can turn a memory into a work of art."

—Jill Person

Approaching outdoor shots requires an intimate understanding of natural light. To make sure that the background colors of the clouds and water could be seen in contrast to the soft peach roses and matching awning we had to properly expose the image. After a late afternoon downpour, we were able to capture the warm dusk horizon—an exquisite backdrop for an event designed by Chad Michael Peters. To highlight the ambience of a reception in an elegant tent, we included walkway lanterns in the frame.

Photograph by Person + Killian Photography

Photograph by Person + Killian Photography

"Capturing the vibrancy of hues and the dynamics of setting and movement showcases raw emotion while preserving the day's atmosphere."

—Laurén Killian

Right: Dana Markos designed the floral arrangement for a dramatic entrance piece that drew guests out of the hallway and into the ballroom at Taj Boston.

Facing page: Utilizing available lighting and flowers for a romantic atmosphere—and inspired by the huppah floral design by William Mizuta—we captured the warmth of the room, bringing in the seasons and taking advantage of different colors. By using such techniques as a shallow depth of field or uplighting, we are able to make images look soft and welcoming and bring out the natural beauty of the scenes.

Photograph by Person + Killian Photography

views

To plan an event that happens without a hitch, hire professionals that you can trust, and be confident that you've hired the right people. With the right group collectively coming together as a team, anything is possible.

BRIAN PHILLIPS PHOTOGRAPHY

BRIAN PHILLIPS | MARIA PHILLIPS

A photograph not only freezes motion, it also draws out the emotions of the moment. Brian Phillips began his career as a freshman in high school when a well-known professional in the photojournalism community invited Brian to assist him in covering a Buffalo Bills football game. This eventually led to a career in journalism. By the time Brian got into the field of event photography, he had the necessary skills to take peak action photos at events and recognized the potential for such skills in the wedding industry.

New England offers a rich environment for photography with a wide range of events, venues, landscapes, and cultural diversity. One day, Brian may cover a high-end function in Boston or Newport then on another day shoot a low-key event at a Maine or Vermont farm. With an abundance of modern and historical structures as well as the ocean and mountains in the region, every day is an adventure that adds to his repertoire of shots. Drawing from experience, Brian pushes his boundaries to do things he's never done before to present a couple with a unique array of memories with the key powerful images that encapsulate the narrative of the day.

For a wedding at the Boston Public Library, I used the staircase in the corner of the room to get the angle I needed to capture the columns, the architecture of the ceiling, the amazing floral pieces in the middle of the room, and the depth of the table—all in one shot.

"Pictures should tell a story incorporating the mood, feeling, and emotions of the special event."

—Brian Phillips

A good shot will utilize dramatic lighting to capture architectural elements and centerpieces and command your eyes around the photograph. Lens selection can accentuate or blur foreground and background features while editing techniques are also helpful to single out key elements of a photograph.

"With a great shot, your eyes will journey around the photograph like it is a map."

—Brian Phillips

Using a fish-eye lens, I was able to utilize subtle curving to show off the overall architecture and lighting of a space. Shooting from above allowed me to capture the band, the motion of the people dancing, and downtown Boston below. Even a centerpiece, replete with the lines and forms of shadow and light, allows for a lavish and elegant photograph.

views

You have to like the images your potential photographer shows you. Look at how an entire event is handled and what the artist is capable of. You should also admire the photographer as a person as well as a professional. If you do not connect, you won't be as comfortable and look your best.

CHERYL RICHARDS, PHOTOGRAPHER
CHERYL RICHARDS

As one of New England's most sought-after photographers, Cheryl Richards captures the excitement of an event with an unobtrusive, sensitive approach. She has traveled as far as Europe, Beverly Hills, and Aspen for people such as Peter Lynch, Jack Welch, Jack Connors, Sam Donaldson, and many other notables.

A multiple *Boston Magazine* "Best of Boston" winner for "Best Wedding Photographer" and noted as the "Pro's Pro," Cheryl deftly blurs the line between shooting still documentaries and creating art. She has had some of the world's most famous faces in front of her lens, including Oprah, Maya Angelou, and the Dalai Lama, yet has the ability to coax out the same senses of regality and playfulness from her subjects. Her amazing eye for people and imagery influences her photographs, while a distinctive, journalistic tone captures natural, spontaneous moments throughout a celebration.

Besides events, Cheryl has proven her talents in fashion and fine art photography. Her passion is black and white film and she enjoys spending time in her darkroom creating pieces worthy of being hung in a museum. Cheryl prefers the romantic, timeless, mysterious qualities it contributes to a subject but of course fully embraces the wonders of digital photography as well. One bride was so enthused by Cheryl's wedding work that she offered to wear a sandwich board promoting her photographer. If that's not artist appreciation, what is?

Almost anyone can take a few good photos these days, but events are so important that all of the photos should be great. With years of experience, instincts, and an ingrained vision for composition and lighting, my goal is to capture emotions to create photos that are unique and priceless.

Photograph by Cheryl Richards

Photograph by Cheryl Richards

Photograph by Cheryl Richards

Photograph by Cheryl Richards

Photograph by Cheryl Richards

"The in-between moments are often the most special."

—Cheryl Richards

When a couple invites me to document their special day I take the responsibility very seriously, and a big part of the success comes from being able to put people at ease so they can be themselves in front of the camera. The day goes by so quickly that I have to be ready for anything, at all times. I'm constantly scanning the room for interesting angles, special interactions, and other unexpected moments that really represent the emotions of the day. Artful photographs are meant to be elegant yet endearing, unobtrusive yet intimate, soulful yet spontaneous, and that's precisely what I aim to capture.

views

Three incredibly important things to remember when choosing your photographer are reputation, genuine personality, and creativity. Since your photographer will be capturing the most intimate moments of your event, you need to know you can trust her to create high-quality images that truly reflect your spirit.

CORRELATION PRODUCTIONS
ROB CORR

Imagine grooving to "99 Luftballons" when suddenly dozens of cherry red balloons begin to fall from the ceiling. Or watching a bride and her father share a touching first dance while, on the screen behind them, photographs of the little girl growing up are intercut with the live camera feed. For the staff at Correlation Productions, simply playing a song isn't enough. Using state-of-the-art equipment and Hollywood-worthy production values, Rob Corr, Craig Jeppesen, and their team of DJs, producers, videographers, and lighting and sound designers create a uniquely interactive mood at every event they're involved with.

Formed by Rob in the mid-'90s, Correlation Productions has since been redefining music and entertainment with a technological approach. Rather than just play a song list, they engage the crowd with props, interactive instructions, and even project people onto the screen. Instead of merely recording an event and editing it later, at least three videographers and an on-site producer capture multiple angles and viewpoints, often projecting them onto a screen in real-time. The process is much like shooting a live television show, and makes it possible to do things like instantly replay a wedding ceremony as the guests arrive for the reception. As much video jockeys as they are DJs, Rob and his crew can manipulate an endless library of music videos and other media just as they would with vinyl and a turntable, delivering the antithesis of a static performance. Expanding into lighting design has made Corr Pros an almost one-stop-shop for professional, jaw-dropping effects and live, interactive entertainment.

I had the pleasure of lighting Cirque USA at a recent event and I was completely astounded. Aerial bartenders, acrobats, clowns and mimes, hula hoop dancers, stilt walkers, and fabric aerialists provide such an incredible palette, and it's a fun challenge to light a room for both event and performance purposes.

Photograph courtesy of Correlation Productions

Photograph courtesy of Correlation Productions

Photograph courtesy of Correlation Productions

"If you continually strive to impress yourself, you will always be proud of what you produce."

—Rob Corr

Right: The advancement of technology has made creativity truly limitless. We used to be restricted in some ways by what our equipment could do, but now we have access to every song, video, commercial, and special effect you could imagine. But what really makes what we do unique is the human component. Without people to continually engage the crowd and draw them in, it's just stale noise through the speakers or a picture on a wall.

Facing page top and bottom left: Our equipment is known for being the best—other lighting designers and even some theater companies rent it out—but I always make sure to have at least one backup of every piece with me at an event. Once I've finished with setup and determined that everything is working properly, if I happen to have a few extra lights I'll hook those up as well. They're not doing any good just sitting in my van, so why not use them to make someone's memorable night even more extraordinary?

Facing page bottom right: We created an '80s-themed video dance party for the students at Yale University, and I think it was unlike anything they'd ever attended before. College kids especially get a kick out of seeing themselves up on a big screen, and when combined with a laser light show, confetti explosions, and music video clips, it's a pretty incredible experience.

Photograph by Michelle Wade Photography

views

Be careful of "weekend warriors." These are entertainers working their full-time jobs during the week and masquerading as professionals on the weekends. Many times with larger companies the person who booked your event will not always be the talent who arrives for your engagement. If it's an individual, they may not have adequate equipment, insurance, or even know how to properly use their own gear. Try to find someone who's as dedicated as you are to making your party fantastic.

"Being involved in a special event is like watching a child go off to kindergarten—it evokes feelings of pride and excitement all wrapped into one."

—Dana Bartone

What we do is not solely wrapped up in the artistry of the hairstyle or the makeup, but it's in the products and the process that we use to implement all of that. We consider the process as important as the look; that's the only way to ensure everything will hold up throughout an event.

Photograph by Carla Ten Eyck Photography

views

Communication with the stylist is key to ensuring the look is gorgeous and that you're happy with the end result. Don't be afraid to say what you want, both before and during the process. Even though they are professionals, you have to trust yourself to know what you want and what you'll be comfortable with.

ENTERTAINMENT SPECIALISTS
MICHAEL AMADO

When Michael Amado was a college radio DJ, record companies from New York City would solicit his honest opinion of their songs by sending him sample records. Those records turned out to be more than just free music—they were connections to an industry that would set Michael on the path to forming his own entertainment company. After working as a promoter for artists and producers such as Russell Simmons, Run DMC, LL Cool J, DJ Jazzy Jeff, and Will Smith, Michael transitioned into the position of musical director of a high-end restaurant. In 1987, he gathered his skills, knowledge, and connections and incorporated Entertainment Specialists.

His background in booking bands hasn't deserted him; today he manages Boston Harbor Hotel's summer concert series, as well as the entertainment for some of the trendiest venues on Martha's Vineyard and in Newport, Rhode Island. But it's the private event work with Entertainment Specialists that lets Michael live out his passion as one of America's most requested DJs, steadily performing nationwide at over 125 events each year.

With the help of senior event planner Barbara Spano, musician and disc jockey John Zucco, booker and manager Toni Bianco, DJ specialist Ron Furr, and Steve Ciccolini—leader of one of the company's most sought-after bands, Double Vision—Entertainment Specialists has come to represent over 200 bands and DJs who perform all across America. Coveted New England bands like The World Premier Band, Manhattan Touch, and New York Minute are available, as are national recording artists such as Jennifer Hudson, Train, Queen Latifah, Michael Bolton, Usher, and many other big name acts.

Our theatrical designers, Everett Hoag and Alexandra Silva, come from the theater industry in Manhattan. With their expertise, we design costumes and characters that have no limits. Our designers have developed such show-stopping creations as living tables and statues, and we represent the most amazing *cirque* performers, professionals who constantly leave guests in amazement.

Photograph by Brian Phillips Photography

Photograph by Brian Phillips Photography

Photograph by Brian Phillips Photography

Photograph by Person + Killian Photography

"Always make your guests wonder
what you're going to do next."
—Michael Amado

Right: I'm what is known as a "turntableist," meaning that when I perform I actually spin records on a turntable "old school NYC style," as opposed to the newer crop of DJs that simply push buttons on a laptop. After 25 years of experience, I still enjoy designing a musical theme that fits the personality of the host and the style of the event.

Facing page: Our New England-based bands have played at some of the most extravagant venues in Miami, New York, Newport, and Boston, including numerous performances at the Kennedy compound in Hyannis Port, and private events for celebrities.

views

I think of being a DJ as comparable to being on the television show "Iron Chef." The chefs have to come up with an innovative dish using only a set list of ingredients. When I DJ an event, I sit down with the hosts and create a list of music for cocktails, dinner, and dancing, with the challenge being to mix that music—like a chef in the kitchen—to produce a masterful blend of music.

GENERATIONS CINEMASTORIES

NAOMI RAISELLE | JACK BROTMAN | LAUREN SCHUMACHER

Capturing real life by blending moving images and live sound is the fine art of cinematic storytelling. GENERATIONS cinemastories is passionate about creating timeless pieces that tell stories about people, their celebrations, and important moments. Using the flexibility of digital media, the studio is equally adept at creating a textured video wall for a party, a modern cinematic love poem for a couple, or a living biography for a special birthday. GENERATIONS cinemastories designs with images from real life. Whether telling a story about a wedding through multi-camera videography or creating a moving montage to coordinate with an event's décor, the studio is dedicated to creatively expressing the human experience.

With collective experience in filmmaking, writing, counseling, DJing, videography, soundtrack design, and improvisation, Jack Brotman, Naomi Raiselle, and Lauren Schumacher form a cohesive team of talent. The studio professionals care as much about how they perform their work as the work they produce. Whether shooting a corporate event, working with an event planner to create a project for a nonprofit, or proposing a customized media package for a bat mitzvah, the team treats every client as its first and every project as a new challenge. While deeply committed to the value of tradition, GENERATIONS cinemestories continues to frame important life events in fresh and unexpected forms.

We often chat with the newly married couple at the end of their wedding reception when most guests have gone. It's the perfect time for the couple to sit with us and reflect on their experiences of the wedding day that is drawing to a close.

"Filmmaking should capture the beauty and natural sound of an event, and then infuse the whole with personal reflection to create depth and meaning."

—Naomi Raiselle

Right: Great storytelling depends on great people skills. While we are usually out of sight, our eyes and ears are always open to notice and capture the in-between moments when magical things just happen.

Facing page: We strive to be relaxed and gracious at events as we want people to relate comfortably to us and not experience camera fear. We may use three, four, or more out-of-sight cameras, and an equal number of wireless mics to deftly capture the movement and sound of a performance, the words and gestures of an intimate wedding, or the colorful excitement at a bat mitzvah celebration. As artistic expressionists, we have the ability to capture motion and emotion in black and white or intense color, painting a picture of life as it is to last forever.

Photograph by Person + Killian Photography

views

Find a videography team you feel relaxed around and who will work harmoniously with your still photographer. Ask yourself "What do I want the final film to express?" Cinematography is more than a series of images set to music, so familiarize yourself with the medium and its creative possibilities. Avoid working with a videographer who uses a template approach. Your event is a totally unique adventure and should be expressed as an original work of art.

GENEVIEVE DE MANIO PHOTOGRAPHY

GENEVIEVE DE MANIO

A truly great photographer knows exactly when to jump in and offer guidance and when to step back and let a magical moment unfold. Walking that fine line between leader and spectator is tricky, but Genevieve de Manio has managed to master it. She's also perfected the art of coaxing gorgeous, funny, touching, and dazzling scenes from guests at events big and small, beautifully reflecting both the posed and the candid.

Not bad for someone who only stumbled upon photography as a way to fulfill an arts credit in college. That chance encounter with the camera awakened inside Genevieve a passion she never knew she had, leading her to study at the Portfolio Center in Atlanta and eventually move to New York City. There she worked with some of the industry's most esteemed portrait and fashion photographers in the commercial circuit. But shortly after moving to Boston, Genevieve became disenchanted with the industry, yearning instead to create pictures that captured a story rather than conveyed a pre-arranged message. After photographing a friend's wedding, she knew she had found her calling.

In 1997 Genevieve opened her own studio, and now produces images that reflect her fine arts aesthetic and discover the stolen moments within a large party. She constantly seeks out new and creative ways to approach an image, putting all her skills to use photographing portraits, intricate details, mouthwatering food, and sweeping panoramic locations. Genevieve knows instantly when she gets that perfect shot, but that doesn't stop her from seeking out the next one.

I find it rewarding to be the creator of something that will be treasured and passed down for generations. Often I will hear that I took the last photograph of an elderly relative, providing the family with both a physical keepsake and the memory of a joyous time.

Photograph by Genevieve de Manio

Photograph by Genevieve de Manio

Photograph by Genevieve de Manio

Photograph by Genevieve de Manio

"A photographer should always have her antenna up, looking for the moments that might otherwise slip away."

—Genevieve de Manio

There are so many moments during an event that slip by so quickly that I consider it my mission to capture as many as possible. I'm drawn to the quiet shots, the times when one or two people are overflowing with the emotions of the moment, such as a bride and groom wrapped in each other's arms on the dance floor for the first time or a father giving his daughter a quick hug during her reception. I'll do anything in my power to find these shots—once I climbed a column to see over the crowd when I was seven months pregnant! I got a lot of funny and concerned looks, but it was worth it for the picture I snapped.

views

Lighting has a tremendous impact on photographs. Keep in mind whatever light you choose to surround yourself and your guests with will be reflected in the images. Most photographers seek out natural light whenever possible as it's more flattering, but artificial colored light from a designer can also make an incredible statement when photographing décor.

MICHELLE WADE PHOTOGRAPHY
MICHELLE WADE

Some photographers will do anything to get the perfect shot, even hang out of speeding cars or risk their own personal safety in busy Times Square. Michelle Wade is one of those adventurers, a woman who will crawl on the ground or scale any available surface if it means the resulting image will be spectacular. Fun and energetic, Michelle maintains that personality creates memorable photographs. When people come to her requesting that she shoot their engagement session, family portrait, or bar mitzvah keepsakes, they are requesting the woman as much as her unique photographic style and body of work.

Through gentle suggestions—a head tilt here, a bouquet adjustment there—Michelle eradicates any trace of camera shy jitters and guides her subjects to natural, emotion-filled poses. Her innate expressiveness immediately puts people at ease, as does her practice of shooting an engagement session with a couple before their big day. Capturing a bride and groom's "first glance" is important to Michelle: the instant when the couple glimpses each other for the first time that day is a moment unlike any other.

Michelle is also an expert in the emerging style of boudoir photography. Tasteful, elegant, and classically sexy images bound together in a bedside book make a sassy gift for any groom, and it's a testament to Michelle's trustworthy persona that so many brides feel so comfortable in her presence.

Using a long lens, especially during weddings, helps people forget that I'm even there. Snapping an intimate moment between newlyweds is so much easier when there's not a camera directly in their faces.

Photograph by Michelle Wade Photography

"A camera is a tool to help capture human emotions."

—Michelle Wade

After graduating from Hallmark Institute of Photography in 2002, I interned with a wedding photographer and knew immediately that this was what I wanted to primarily focus on. Photographing the energy and love of that day is something so special and intimate. I feel honored every time I'm welcomed into a family and allowed to document their milestones, from engagement to wedding to children and beyond.

views

Make sure your photographer explains exactly what you will receive at the conclusion of your event, whether it's albums, discs, online images, or a combination. There are so many different ways to share photographs nowadays that the standard wedding portrait may not be the main focus anymore. Know what you will be taking with you to treasure.

Murray Hill Talent
CORY HARDING | PAUL NATALE | CORIN ASHLEY

When three good friends turned a midcentury ice cream cone factory into a state-of-the-art sound stage for rehearsal and recording, they transformed more than a building. They re-invented the traditional talent agency model by cutting out the proverbial middleman in favor of being true resources to party hosts and planners. To develop the right aural and visual vibe for the occasion, the musicians distill countless options into tailored recommendations—the best band, music, wardrobe, and so on—and will tweak the composition of existing bands or create new ones as needed.

The cofounders of Murray Hill Talent—Cory Harding, Paul Natale, and Corin Ashley—go way back, so they understand and embrace each other's personalities and strengths. Before establishing their Massachusetts-based company, the musicians and songwriters worked as business professionals in the music industry and toured together as a band. At Murray Hill Talent, guitarist Cory, the company's resident Berklee College of Music graduate, is responsible for developing relationships with bands and performers; singer Paul oversees internal operations and focuses on the DJ roster; and bassist-vocalist Corin heads up musical planning and creative conceptualization. These guys embody the concept of synergy.

Cory, Paul, and Corin have yet to meet a musical genre that doesn't interest them. Sure, they have their favorites, but their company's repertoire is insanely diverse—alternative to classical, Americana to Flamenco, Celtic, and Indian—which gives them infinite options for customizing each performance.

For a Hartford Hospital fundraising gala, we developed a '60s vintage soul theme from set list to wardrobe. Even though the venue wasn't set up for dancing, our band Flipside's music was so lively that people rushed the stage and danced anyway.

Photograph by Murray Hill Talent

"The right song at the right time can change a person's life."

—Cory Harding

Think about some of the best concerts you've attended. What likely made them special is how hard the performers were working in every precise moment; they weren't playing to an empty room, they were playing to a totally captivated crowd. An audience's positive energy profoundly impacts the artists, so listeners are indirectly participating in the process of creating music. We love being based in New England because it's a vibrant music scene and has incredible regional diversity, which allows us to explore all genres and perform in groups of all sizes. One of our more modern concept bands, Solstice, is a hybrid of musicians improvising over down-tempo beats that produces a fresh cosmopolitan ambience. There's no rewind button with live music, which is exactly what makes each event so interesting.

views

Don't be afraid to try something new, because nobody ever got anywhere interesting by just following the leader. When you're thinking about the music for a special event, it's a good idea to consider not only raw talent but also experience, since the nature of live performances means that musicians often have to think on their toes.

SIMAN ENTERTAINMENT
DARREN SIMAN | AUDRA SIMAN

Say goodbye to the typical cookie-cutter bands and DJs of yesterday, and welcome the artists and management of Siman Entertainment. Since 2000, husband-and-wife team Darren and Audra Siman have been turning the heads of hosts and industry A-listers with their own unique brand of energetic bands, DJs, and eclectic small groups. Rooted in their own love of music, Darren and Audra have devised a new style of entertainment, one that is based on the look and sound of today, yet appeals to a multigenerational audience.

Siman Entertainment focuses on modernizing the music with a group of artistic performers who capture the emotion behind the sound. During a Siman Entertainment wedding ceremony, guests will lose themselves in the lush music of Coldplay and Snow Patrol alongside the traditional sounds of Handel and Mozart. Stylish cocktail hours are infused with the lounge-style electronica of The ReMix Concept. During the party, even the stiffest of dancers won't be able to resist the hip-shaking grooves of The Superband, Bounce, and Simon Sez.

Beginning at each note, Siman Entertainment carefully crafts the perfect combination of musicians, singers, and DJs around the host's personality and vision. A live showcase allows the host the opportunity to hear a variety of musical options during the planning process. Behind each event, Siman Entertainment's experienced guidance ensures a seamless backdrop of signature music.

To follow the trends of today's music, bands that include multiple horns, strings, and singers are no longer a necessity. Instead, smaller groups of six to eight multifaceted musicians make up the modern band. During the "From Inspiration to Reality" photo shoot at The Loft in Boston for the Style Me Pretty blog, the singers of The Superband channel the classic look and sound of the 1950s.

Photograph by Jorge Mayer Photography

Photograph by Eric Laurits

Photograph by Jennifer Doumato Lamy, Zenobia Photography Studios

"An event is happening now, not 30 years ago, so the music needs to be updated to fit the current generation."

—Darren Siman

Every celebration or event is different and requires a unique sound to bring about just the right ambience. Even the different portions of an event, from the cocktail hour to the dancing to the after-party, may call for their own style of music. Our goal is to put together the band, DJ, or combination of the two that will best fit the personality of the host and the party. The cool factor of Bounce, the pop hooks of The Superband, and the Best of Both Worlds live musician/DJ are just a few of the artists we offer.

views

Other options outside the traditional party music genre do exist, starting with an entire subset of musicians who are in tune with the music of the current generation. They bring an entirely new style of music to the event industry, which is refreshing. That doesn't mean that they forget about the classics or other traditional songs. They just modernize them a bit and make them more meaningful to the guests.

Art of Celebration

NEW ENGLAND TEAM
Associate Publisher: Laureen Edelson
Graphic Designer: Paul Strength
Editor: Lindsey Wilson
Production Coordinator: Drea Williams

HEADQUARTERS TEAM
Publisher: Brian G. Carabet
Publisher: John A. Shand
Executive Publisher: Phil Reavis
Publication & Circulation Manager: Lauren B. Castelli
Senior Graphic Designer: Emily A. Kattan
Graphic Designer: Kendall Muellner
Managing Editor: Rosalie Z. Wilson
Editor: Anita M. Kasmar
Editor: Jennifer Nelson
Editor: Sarah Tangney
Managing Production Coordinator: Kristy Randall
Project Coordinator: Laura Greenwood
Traffic Coordinator: Katrina Autem
Administrative Manager: Carol Kendall
Client Support Coordinator: Amanda Mathers

PANACHE PARTNERS, LLC
CORPORATE HEADQUARTERS
1424 Gables Court
Plano, TX 75075
469.246.6060
www.panache.com
www.panachecelebrations.com

INDEX

THE PANACHE COLLECTION

CREATING SPECTACULAR PUBLICATIONS FOR DISCERNING READERS

Dream Homes Series
An Exclusive Showcase of the Finest Architects, Designers and Builders

Carolinas
Chicago
Coastal California
Colorado
Deserts
Florida
Georgia
Los Angeles
Metro New York
Michigan
Minnesota
New England

New Jersey
Northern California
Ohio & Pennsylvania
Pacific Northwest
Philadelphia
South Florida
Southwest
Tennessee
Texas
Washington, D.C.

Spectacular Homes Series
An Exclusive Showcase of the Finest Interior Designers

California
Carolinas
Chicago
Colorado
Florida
Georgia
Heartland
London
Michigan
Minnesota
New England

Metro New York
Ohio & Pennsylvania
Pacific Northwest
Philadelphia
South Florida
Southwest
Tennessee
Texas
Toronto
Washington, D.C.
Western Canada

Perspectives on Design Series
Design Philosophies Expressed by Leading Professionals

California
Carolinas
Chicago
Colorado
Florida
Georgia
Great Lakes
London

Minnesota
New England
New York
Pacific Northwest
South Florida
Southwest
Western Canada

Art of Celebration Series
The Making of a Gala

Chicago & the Greater Midwest
Georgia
New England
New York
South Florida
Southern California
Southern Style
Southwest
Toronto
Washington, D.C.
Wine Country

Spectacular Wineries Series
A Captivating Tour of Established, Estate and Boutique Wineries

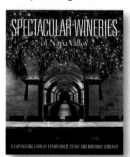

California's Central Coast
Napa Valley
New York
Sonoma County
Texas

Specialty Titles
The Finest in Unique Luxury Lifestyle Publications

21st Century Homes
Cloth and Culture: Couture Creations of Ruth E. Funk
Distinguished Inns of North America
Experience British Columbia
Extraordinary Homes California
Geoffrey Bradfield Ex Arte
Interiors Southeast
Into the Earth: A Wine Cave Renaissance
Shades of Green Tennessee
Spectacular Golf of Colorado
Spectacular Golf of Texas
Spectacular Hotels
Spectacular Restaurants of Texas
Visions of Design

City by Design Series
An Architectural Perspective

Atlanta
Charlotte
Chicago
Dallas
Denver
Orlando
Phoenix
San Francisco
Texas

PanacheCelebrations.com
Where the Event Industry's Finest Professionals Gather, Share, and Inspire

PanacheCelebrations.com overflows with innovative ideas from leading event planners, designers, caterers, and other specialists. A gallery of photographs and library of advice-oriented articles are among the comprehensive site's offerings.

Panache Partners, LLC   1424 Gables Court   Plano, Texas 75075   469.246.6060   www.panache.com